THE REBEL
NEGOTIATOR'S
GUIDE
TO
GETTING
A
RAISE

ISBN: 978-0-578-51755-1

TABLE OF CONTENTS

FOREWORD

I have always been amazed at how much the average person fears negotiation. Many see it as a battle full of screaming, yelling, and fist-pounding, where neither party walks away happy. I, however, look at negotiation as a puzzle and an opportunity to influence people to reach an agreement.

I teach negotiation workshops all over the world. As a member of the Negotiation Center of Excellence for one of the world's largest IT and consulting services providers, I teach these workshops to help participants understand their strengths and weaknesses as negotiators, enhance their negotiation acumen, remain self-aware at the negotiating table, and fine-tune their use of negotiation methodology that can be utilized in a principled and disciplined way.

I strictly adhere to the "4x7" approach—four principles and seven elements—that affects the success of every negotiation, personal and professional. On Day 1 of the workshop, I introduce this approach in a variety of different transactional contexts, most of which we have all experienced. The first volume in *The Rebel Negotiator's Guide To…* series was focused on negotiating the purchase of a new car, which can be an anxiety and stress-laden experience, even for experienced negotiators. This book addresses another transaction which can be just as challenging and even terrifying for some—getting a raise.

My approach for negotiating a raise is built on the same methodology that is the foundation for the $5 billion in consulting, technology, and outsourcing agreements that I have successfully negotiated during my career. Although anxiety, stress, and high blood pressure seem to be table stakes in a salary negotiation, I will prepare you for an experience that is less traumatic and, perhaps, even pleasant.

As we begin this journey, it is important to be mindful of macroeconomic indicators and how their performance and trends may impact the outcome of the salary negotiation. Let's recap a bit to understand current conditions. Since 2009, the global economy has strengthened significantly, and unemployment has fallen to historically low levels. It is common to hear employers talk about their challenges in attracting and retaining quality talent. In other words, a war for talent has emerged as certain skills and abilities are in high demand. These conditions all suggest a salary increase should be ripe for the picking, especially if some of those skills fit squarely within your area of expertise.

However, there are other forces at work that are generating some headwind in this process. According to Korn Ferry, the global organizational consulting and talent acquisition firm, professionals in the early stages of their careers in 14 of the 18 largest world economies earn less now—on an inflation-adjusted basis—than they did 10 years ago. Why are we failing to see more correlation between the thriving economy and the size of our paychecks?

The answer as to why wages are not maintaining pace with the global economy is unclear. Some attribute it to the fact that many companies became extremely conservative during the 2008 financial crisis and have maintained that level of discipline ever since. Others suggest that the workers who were laid off in the 2008 recession found new jobs which paid them a lower salary. Some blame robotic process automation or artificial intelligence which has been deployed to perform processes and tasks that were previously performed by highly compensated workers. Others point to the continued trend to take advantage of labor arbitrage and off-shore work to less costly locations. Finally, some cite demographic patterns for this wage disparity as baby boomers are delaying retirement and staying in the workforce much longer than anticipated.

In a November 19, 2018, article in *Briefings Magazine*, writer Chris Taylor suggests the answer has nothing to do with automation, offshoring, unemployment rates, or any major business disruption. Rather, he suggests that, "Many organizations are taking a more holistic view of compensation, looking well beyond the actual paycheck to more time off, more elaborate healthcare benefits, or other perks in lieu of salary increases." I, for one, am not a proponent of the holistic approach and am standing firmly in the camp with the 50% of my fellow Americans who have expressed through a variety of surveys that they feel underpaid.

While the broader economy may have some detrimental impact on your ability to secure the salary increase you are seeking, I believe the silver bullet in this negotiation comes in the form of legitimacy. Your success in this negotiation will hinge upon your ability to remain principled and disciplined and to focus on the legitimacy that supports the raise you are seeking. We will focus on legitimacy in more detail. In the meantime, remember the following quote by Professor of Pathology Edwin R. Fisher when addressing a Congressional subcommittee in 1978: "In God we trust; all others must bring the data."

As you read this book, you can take comfort in the fact that I have cut my teeth and inflicted plenty of wounds at the negotiating table over the past twenty years with some of the most difficult and aggressive negotiators on the planet—*Fortune* 500 buyers and their procurement organizations, elite law firms, and third-party advisory firms. I have also had ample experience in salary negotiations with superiors who thought they had a more legitimate understanding of the market-relevant salary for the role in which I was serving, and value I was delivering, to the organization. Unfortunately, many of those experiences were extremely frustrating as they included inexperienced negotiators and inferior negotiation processes.

On the inexperience issue, it is important to remember there is no correlation between serving in a senior level role in an organization and negotiation acumen. The development and fine-tuning of negotiation skills is generally overlooked in all levels of our educational system and is not taught when you enter the business world or your profession of choice. I am amazed such an important skill that impacts every aspect of our personal and professional lives receives so little attention.

I am sure you have all uttered the words, "I wish I knew then what I know now" and for me, that quote applies perfectly to my negotiation skills. I can attest to the fact that in my undergraduate, graduate, and law school curriculum, there was no focus on developing and fine-tuning my strengths and weaknesses as a negotiator and I believe my experience is typical. Yet, it is amazing how many people rate themselves as "experts" when it comes to negotiation skills. Unfortunately, those expert ratings could not be further from the truth for most respondents. It is my frustration with the tendency to over-inflate negotiation skills that inspired me to lead a rebellion focused on achieving effective and efficient negotiations and made me proud to earn the title, "The Rebel Negotiator." Hopefully, the self-anointed experts will buy this book, read it in a clandestine manner, adopt its principles, and legitimately, with a lot of practice and effort, earn the "expert" moniker they have been claiming for years.

After you read this book and are seated in the chair across from your boss, I strongly encourage you to focus on the 4x7 approach methodology, remain principled and disciplined, focus on legitimacy, separate the substance of the negotiation from any relationship with the other party, refrain from reacting out of fear, and channel your inner Rebel Negotiator. Ultimately, that approach should allow you to feel confident throughout the negotiation and to achieve an outcome that meets your key interest in this process, being paid a legitimate and market-relevant salary consistent with your skillset and the value you deliver on a daily basis. Depending upon your level of success, maybe you will take some of the proceeds and indulge in whatever makes you happy.

For those of you who are generally quick to cave in or like to split the difference, be mindful of the fact that a few thousand dollars difference in base salary can have a significant impact over time. For a new employee, negotiating a salary offer up by $5,000 can have a material impact over the course of his career. A 25-year-old employee who enters the job market at $55,000 versus an employee who fails to negotiate and accepts a salary of

$50,000 will earn approximately $600,000 more over the course of a 40-year career assuming a 5% annual increase over that term. Therefore, prepare diligently for the salary negotiation as success will have a lasting impact.

IT'S TIME TO FACE REALITY

It is highly likely that at some point in your adult life you may have said these words:

1. I am being taken advantage of.

2. I am working for pennies on the dollar.

3. All of my peers at (insert company name) are making more than I am.

4. Another day of indentured servitude.

5. I should definitely be making more money than (insert peer name)

6. Another year of no base salary increases. How wonderful.

7. We overachieved on revenue and profit. Why is the bonus pool not being funded at 100%?

8. I need to make more money!

9. I am undervalued as an employee.

10. I work way too hard for a measly 2% salary increase.

11. Everyone makes more than I do. It's just not fair.

12. Why am I working so hard?

13. It's time to make a change.

14. I need to update my resume.

15. What work/life balance?

No matter which statement you made, you probably decided this: It's time to get a raise. As we begin to execute against that objective, let's review a few facts about our professional lives:

1. The average American spends 90,000 hours at work over his lifetime.

2. 87% of Americans have no passion for their jobs.

3. 80% of U.S. workers are outright dissatisfied with their jobs.

4. Nearly 60% of those workers claim their jobs are making them insomniacs.

5. The average American spends more than 100 hours commuting every year.

6. 25% of Americans say work is their number one source of stress.

7. A third of the managers in the United Kingdom report they

are losing their sense of humor because of work.

8. Nearly half of Americans have gained weight at their current jobs—26% have gained more than 10 pounds, and 11% have gained more than 20 pounds.

9. Most Americans fail to use all of their vacation days—there were some 705 million unused days off last year alone.

10. 40% of millennials feel guilty for using all of their vacation days.

11. When employees do take vacation, 42% feel pressured to check in while they are away.

12. 89% of U.S. workers believe they deserve a raise but only 54% plan to ask for one.

In a survey conducted by staffing firm Robert Half, workers preferred house cleaning, a root canal, and an IRS audit to asking for a raise.

While this book can't help you lose weight, speed up your commute, minimize how much time you spend in the office, or limit how many times a day you check your email while on vacation, it will provide you with a negotiation strategy and framework to assist in your endeavor to be paid a market-relevant and legitimate wage for the 90,000 hours you will spend at work during your lifetime.

You likely made the decision to get a raise with plenty of conviction in your voice and a high level of excitement, as the possibilities seemed endless— more base salary, more bonus, more perks or other fringe benefits, more vacation time, tuition reimbursement for that degree you are interested in pursuing, no more flying in coach, participation in more external training courses, a company car, a trip to the annual executive retreat, or whatever else might satisfy your desire to be paid more, whether in quantifiable hard dollar form or in intangible fringe benefits like those just referenced. Given the amount of time we spend at work, nothing feels more satisfying than knowing you are being paid a market-relevant and legitimate salary for your efforts. The feeling that comes from seeing those additional Benjamins flow into your bank account is heavenly.

Once the excitement wears off and you realize the importance of the task at hand, feelings of stress and anxiety usually surface. Do these comments sound familiar?:

1. I hate asking my boss for anything, let alone more money. She is so difficult to communicate with.

2. The process is too complicated—there are simply too many options and the outcome too ambiguous.

3. I want to avoid the entire negotiation process.

4. I am afraid to negotiate. I feel anxious when I ask for something I want.

5. I am not a good negotiator. I find the entire process to be difficult, scary, agonizing, and overwhelming.

6. It takes me a long time to work up the courage to ask for something I want.

7. I am nervous and stressed out about asking for a raise.

8. She will probably say no, and then what am I going to do?

9. I feel trapped once I walk into her office. The conversation never seems to flow the way I anticipated. When I get off track, I don't make good decisions.

10. I really don't like my boss. She is always so defensive when discussing these types of issues.

11. Even if we agree on an increase, I never feel like I am getting a good deal.

12. I don't feel like my boss is being honest with me. She always has some excuse why she can't give me what I want, even if we both agree it is legitimate.

13. I have a great relationship with my boss. I don't want to jeopardize that.

14. I will work harder this year. My boss will realize my effort and accomplishments and give me a raise. That way, I won't have to ask for anything.

15. Can I just call the Rebel Negotiator to negotiate on my behalf?

Fear of, or the desire to avoid negotiation is typical. In the negotiation workshops I facilitate, I try to understand the level of comfort people have with negotiation, in general, and, specifically, with negotiating a raise.

Workshop participants' feedback about their level of comfort with negotiation consistently focused on these four key areas: (1) a general aversion to conflict, and negotiation for many people is the epitome of conflict; (2) a fear of losing or a fear of hurting the relationship with the other party; (3) a fear of being in an ambiguous situation where the outcome is unclear; and (4) an inability or reluctance to ask for things, which results in lost opportunities for negotiation.

If we think about those four areas in the context of asking for a raise, the level of discomfort grows exponentially. Going to meet with your boss to negotiate a raise can yield plenty of conflict on both sides of the negotiating table. Tempers may flare, relationships may be damaged, and it is not uncommon to leave the table unhappy. As for the fear of losing, people want to feel like they got a "good deal," and that is not always true once the negotiation is completed, the next paycheck arrives, and the dust has settled. Just like when buying a new car, the outcome is so ambiguous given the variability in salary and other terms that we never really know if we achieved a good outcome. Finally, and most importantly, many individuals seeking a raise are reluctant to consider their full range of options. They underestimate their negotiating strength, fail to arm themselves with the necessary data to support the legitimacy of their request, and miss opportunities to capture that elusive "good deal."

Let's be clear: The Internet has played a significant role in facilitating this process. Employees in all industries and at all hierarchical levels have tremendous amounts of data at their fingertips via their desktop, smartphone, or tablet, and many are using this information to their advantage in negotiations. A quick Internet search can reveal legitimate salary data that is segregated by organization size and type, role, years of experience, education level, professional or technical certification, and geographic location. Long gone are the days when salary was secretive; there are websites in which actual salary data is listed by company and hierarchical level, and the millennial generation does not seem to have an issue in disclosing their salary data. To maintain parity among peers, some employers are focusing on maintaining tight salary bands for similarly situated roles. Others are going so far as publishing a salary roster to promote a fundamental sense of fairness across the organization. Ultimately, this focus on transparency could mitigate the lost productivity that may result if material salary gaps among peers serving in similar roles became known.

Many resources are available to determine the market-relevancy of your current salary, including reviewing competitor job postings, speaking with local recruiters to gauge salary ranges for positions they are seeking to fill, talking with peers or colleagues who are engaged in a similar role, and reviewing Securities and Exchange Commission and other governmental filings. Simply search for "Salary Data," and you will be overwhelmed with the amount of data you can access to properly prepare you for the salary negotiation.

While this data is readily available, many individuals fail to use it to their advantage as they become overly anxious or nervous about the negotiation and conveniently use one of the fifteen excuses above to delay the conversation and perpetuate the problem and their frustration. While the Internet provides ample data to assist you in this process, many people are simply too afraid and unwilling to have a difficult conversation.

The bottom line is all the legitimate data in the world won't help if you fear the negotiation. The key is to diligently prepare for the negotiation by arming yourself with legitimacy and to remain agile as it unfolds. By doing so, you will be able to quickly adapt if the negotiation doesn't play out exactly as scripted once you cross the threshold of your boss's office. As the great boxer Mike Tyson famously said, "Everyone has a plan until they get punched in the mouth."

In the spirit of that comment, this book will not focus on the vast amounts of data or the extensive number of websites available that will arm you with the legitimate and market-relevant salary data you will need for the negotiation. Unfortunately, you can have all the data you need and still fail when it's time for the negotiation. Instead, this book will provide you with a framework that will help you as you navigate through the negotiation. Irrespective of your hierarchical role, current salary, years of experience, or any other variable you might think makes you different, my recipe to become a successful negotiator will help you safely navigate through this process.

So, don't be anxious. Let the stress go away. The Rebel Negotiator is here to guide you through each step of the way.

LET'S STICK TO THE RECIPE

"What does negotiation mean to you?" When I ask this question of workshop participants, the feedback makes it appear as if I had asked about combat tactics. They generally describe negotiation as preparing for war—an adversarial process typically marked by screaming and yelling, fist pounding, trench warfare, and, ultimately, winning at all costs. As you prepare for your salary increase negotiation, I encourage you to think of negotiation as a puzzle, not a battle. To help you change your point of view, I am giving you a recipe for becoming a successful negotiator. It has four key ingredients which must be properly mixed to achieve a "desirable" outcome: (1) the ability to influence others; (2) a strong mental and situational awareness; (3) a methodology and process used in a principled and disciplined way; and (4) a willingness to have a difficult conversation. Just like any other good recipe, it is both simple and complex and usually requires fine-tuning to get the final product just right.

"Desirable" in the salary increase context does not necessarily mean you follow the recipe and cash in on the results a few hours later. As I like to say, negotiation, like life, is not always rainbows and lollipops. Getting a desirable outcome requires hard work and time and is likely to force you to operate outside of your comfort zone.

Before I begin to explain each key ingredient, I encourage you to pick an overall negotiation strategy you will rely on as you endeavor to get a raise. When selecting your strategy, think of the importance of the substance of the negotiation and the relationship you want to maintain with the other party to the negotiation.

When negotiating the purchase of a new car or a house, the substance of the negotiation is critical as these are some of the largest purchases you will make in your life. However, maintaining an on-going relationship with the other party is not important as you will likely never see that person again during your lifetime. These negotiations are nothing more than transactional interactions, so your strategy to focus purely on the substance of the negotiation will be sacrosanct. You will not be influenced by or let the relationship with the other party impact your decision making throughout the negotiation process. If you don't like the terms of the agreement, then you can find another house or go to another car dealership.

I will discuss the best alternative to a negotiated agreement—known as BATNA—later, but it is important to understand how your overall negotiation strategy and your BATNA can be impacted by the relationship you want to maintain with the other party to the negotiation. You will never have a stronger BATNA than when you are buying a car. The Rebel Negotiator will never worry about his relationship with a car salesperson, and the list of dealerships he has left mid-negotiation is very long. It is my hope that when you are engaged in a transactional negotiation, you will be laser-focused on the substance of the negotiation and emulate my behavior as necessary.

Compare the house or car negotiation with your daily interaction at the local coffee house, trying to navigate through a busy intersection without any stop lights, or deciding who will enter the elevator first in the crowded lobby of a building. In these types of transactions, the substance is not nearly as important as buying a house or a car, but you are still not concerned about the importance of the on-going relationship with the other party. While you may encounter the other party on a more frequent basis than the house or car transaction, you can always get your coffee elsewhere, take a different route to work, or take the stairs. For these types of negotiations, your strategy is simply tacit coordination.

Pause for a moment and compare the car salesperson, the barista, the stranger in the elevator lobby, or the nameless person in the other car who didn't properly yield at the intersection with your boss. It is likely your boss is someone you engage with daily and who has a significant amount of influence over your job satisfaction and career trajectory. To be blunt, your boss can probably make your life miserable if that was her objective. Based upon the 90,000 hours we will spend at work in our lifetimes, she will have ample time to carry out this objective. Therefore, when engaging with your boss, it is critical to focus both on the substance of the negotiation as well as the importance of the on-going relationship.

There may be instances where you are engaged with your boss where the substance of the negotiation is not important. For example, let's assume you walk up to the photocopier machine to pick up a report you just printed. You see your boss just printed something as well and you pass right by her office on the way back to yours. You decide to drop off her printout on the way. In this instance, your negotiation strategy was focused purely on relationship building, as the substance was relatively unimportant, but the act of service of hand-delivering her printout likely had a positive impact on the relationship.

Now let's focus on the salary negotiation. This is an instance where the substance of the negotiation—you want more money—and the on-going relationship—you must maintain a good working relationship with your boss—are both incredibly important. So, unlike the car or house buying experience, the on-going relationship with the other party will likely influence the outcome of the negotiation. It is in this type of negotiation that we will follow a balanced concerns strategy. We will be mindful of the substance of the negotiation and our relationship with the other party, remain principled and disciplined in our approach and maximize legitimacy, be firm in our interests but flexible in terms of options to meet those interests, and most importantly stay unconditionally constructive.

Unlike the car buying experience, we will not have the pleasure of pounding our fists on the table, grabbing a handful of Otis Spunkmeyer cookies, and heading to another dealership in search of a better deal. With that said, we will not make an uninformed or poor decision solely because of the relationship. I have always said a relationship allows the parties to a negotiation to have an honest and candid conversation. It shouldn't preclude you from obtaining a market-relevant and legitimate salary increase.

Let's confirm that your negotiation strategy is one of balanced concerns, where the substance of the negotiation—the raise—is important, as is the relationship with your boss and employer. Your mission, should you choose to accept it, is to find the proper balance as you navigate through the process. Ultimately, your goal is to emerge from the negotiation with a raise in hand and relationships intact.

YOU AGREE WITH ME, RIGHT?

Influence is the first ingredient in the recipe to becoming a successful negotiator and refers to the ability to have an effect on the character, development, or behavior of someone or something. Negotiation is the exercise of influence and we do this every day. As we discussed previously, daily negotiation could be tacitly coordinating who will enter a door or an elevator, interacting with the coffee barista or waiter to make sure that your drink or lunch is prepared the way you like it, or building a relationship with a family member. An important client negotiation takes into account the concerns of all parties. If you don't like to negotiate or don't believe you are good at it, I challenge you to think about how many times each day you successfully influence and "negotiate" with people around you.

How do you influence your boss to agree with what you believe or want? Your first choice may be to use logic to persuade her. Although logic may lead to a successful outcome, you should realize that despite the preexisting relationship you have, your boss may not want to accept your logic as rational. If this happens, support your reasoning with as much legitimacy as you can to justify your perspective. Legitimacy will likely include much of the readily available and market-relevant salary data we discussed previously.

If this approach doesn't work, you could try to influence the other party through other means that may include socializing with that party or appealing to the relationship. By attempting to build upon your level of affiliation with your boss, you may get her to agree or cooperate with you on issues in the negotiation. You could appeal based upon the relationship by saying something like, "After all we have been through together, all of the long nights and hard work, all of the successes and some failures, and all of the great times, I think I have earned, and I think you owe me this increase. While building upon your level of affiliation may be a good option when you have a good relationship with your boss, that is unfortunately not always the case.

You could decide to influence your boss by trying to engage her in the process—in essence, to build her a golden bridge. Even if your boss is the CEO, she also has a boss, most likely the Board of Directors, and assuming you are delivering value and making her look good, she likely doesn't want you to leave and go to a competitor. So, if your influence and persuasion are not working, think of what Tom Cruise said in the movie *Jerry Maguire*: "Help me help you."

If your efforts are unsuccessful, you can always use negative-influence techniques, including manipulating (lies and deceit), intimidating (loud and abrasive verbal aggressiveness), avoiding (doing nothing), or threatening (comply with what I want, or else). These techniques, however, may mislead other parties or cause them to act against their best interests or wishes. If you want to use these techniques when engaging with your boss, they would sound something like this:

Avoiding: "I have provided ample legitimacy to support the basis for my salary increase. I think I am going to take some much-needed vacation. If you want to meet my salary demand, I am available on my mobile phone. I really hope I hear from you before I return."

Manipulating: "I am really disappointed that you don't find my request to be reasonable. As I mentioned, it is based upon objective, measurable, and verifiable market-relevant salary data for someone with similar experience performing a similar role. I am having dinner tonight with my peers at

Competitor Corporation and am going to share my demand with them and see how it stacks up against their compensation plan. They have been trying to get me to leave for years but I have repeatedly told them how loyal I am to you and our company."

Intimidating: "I can't believe how poorly you are treating me in this process. I have been a valued and loyal employee for many years. I simply want to be compensated in a fair and market-relevant manner, and I am disappointed with how you have handled this process. Imagine what all of those new hires in orientation would think if they knew they would not get a base salary increase for the next three years. Or if they did get an increase, it would not even be consistent with the cost of living."

Threatening: "If you don't give me a salary increase consistent with the terms I am demanding, I will make sure to tell everyone how a loyal and devoted employee like myself is treated after so many years of service. I will also tell all of my colleagues what to expect when they want a raise and to consider other employment options. Finally, I will make sure that my 50,000 Twitter followers, 1,478 LinkedIn Connections, and thousands of Facebook friends will never consider working for this company."

A Note of Caution: A threat of this type may result in you being promptly terminated, so temper the message unless you have a strong BATNA and are ready to immediately execute against it.

The influence ingredient of the successful negotiator recipe is extremely important. Depending on the situation, you can determine how to best influence the other party to agree with you. Hopefully, your approach to negotiation will use logic or social methods, but you can use negative-influence techniques carefully, if needed.

ARE YOU PAYING ATTENTION?

The second key ingredient in the recipe to becoming a successful negotiator is to stay very disciplined, and the best way to do that is by understanding the situation and how effective you are at the negotiating table. These variables are always in motion and they must be fine-tuned during the negotiation.

First, let's first talk about situational awareness, or spotting the game you're playing. Spotting the game is very important because it will dictate the outcome and success of the negotiation. Key questions asked in this game-spotting analysis are these:

1.   Have the parties effectively defined the issues?

2.   Have the parties clearly articulated their interests?

3.   Have the parties considered the full range of options?

4.   Have the parties used objective, measurable, and verifiable standards to develop the options?

5.   Have the parties discussed their alternatives and what will happen if the parties can't reach an agreement?

6. Who is making commitments in the negotiation? Is it one-sided?

7. Is the relationship affecting the negotiation? Are any of the parties being manipulated?

8. How is the communication flow? Are the parties listening or talking past each other? Are they treating each other with respect? Are they attacking the issues or the people at the table?

When you have spotted the game, you can then decide if you want to continue playing the same game, if you want to change it, or if you want to stop playing altogether. Examples of games you don't want to play when trying to get a raise include bidding against yourself, bargaining that results in compromise, caving in because you feel heavily invested in the process, playing chicken, rewarding anchoring, or making decisions based on your perceived level of entrapment. The bottom line is you should never react only to what the other side is doing.

Because it is important for you to have strong situational awareness and avoid participating in a game you don't want to play, I want to go through each of these following scenarios in detail.

Let's start with bidding against yourself. In this scenario, you make commitments and concessions with little or no feedback from your boss. If you've watched the TV show *Pawn Stars*, you know what this looks like. The dialogue in the getting a raise context would sound something like this:

> **Employee:** I have done a lot of market research regarding my current compensation level. I have looked at positions like mine at many of our key competitors and elsewhere in the marketplace. I have focused on individuals with similar years of experience, educational backgrounds, and technical certifications. I have also reviewed several highly regarded annual salary guides and surveys that provide salary data by role, industry, and geography. The

research consistently indicates that my base salary is well below the market average. I also continue to overachieve on my performance targets and have done so on a consistent basis for the past three years. Given the legitimate market data I referenced, which I have copied for our discussion today, I am seeking a base salary increase of 10% or $10,000.

Boss: That seems like a very substantial increase, especially given my budget challenges this year.

Employee: OK. I understand the budget challenges. How about $7,000?

Boss: That is a little more reasonable but is still a lot of money given our financial plan for the year. I will also have to see if that size of an increase even fits within the salary band for your current level and within our compensation policy.

Employee: I realize that is a lot more than any increase I have received in the past few years. I don't want to make you ask for an exception to the policy. How about $5,000?

Boss: Well, that is much more reasonable and within my approval threshold. I think we are close to an agreement on this.

Employee: Well the minimum I will accept is $4,000.

Boss: I understand. Let me check with Human Resources, and I will get back in touch next week. I hope you know how valuable you are to my team. We will get this resolved.

Let's think about what happened in this negotiation for an annual salary increase where the amount being requested seems to be legitimate and market-relevant. The employee has taken a 60 percent haircut for what he believed was market-relevant, and the boss has not yet made a commitment.

The only person making commitments in this exchange is the employee. Here, the employee needs to slow down and run through the eight questions I identified above. When the employee has asked those questions and has "spotted the game," he can adjust his approach accordingly. *Figure 1 shows a diagram of what bidding against yourself looks like.*

FIGURE 1

BIDDING AGAINST YOURSELF

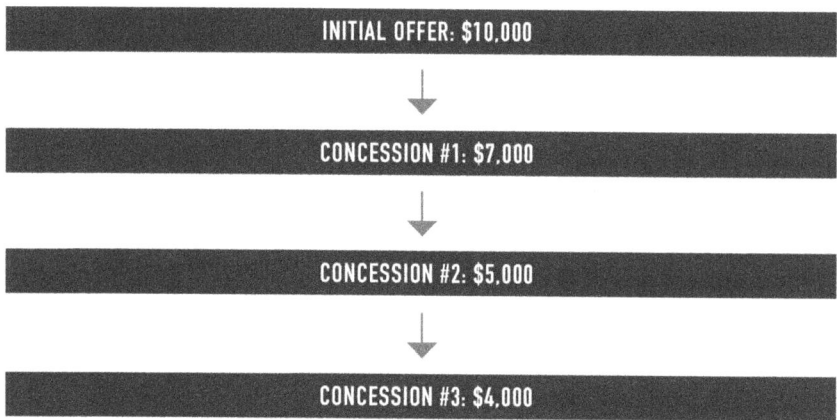

INITIAL OFFER: $10,000

↓

CONCESSION #1: $7,000

↓

CONCESSION #2: $5,000

↓

CONCESSION #3: $4,000

Now let's look at classic traditional bargaining that results in a compromise. If you are a fan of compromise, you should look carefully at its definition. Compromise is an agreement or a settlement of a dispute, which is reached by each side making concessions, to accept standards that are less than desirable. From the Rebel Negotiator's perspective, this is not a good result. I would much rather collaborate with the party on the other side of the table.

The dialogue for traditional bargaining would sound like this:

Employee: I have done a lot of market research regarding my current compensation level. I have looked at positions like mine at many of our key competitors and elsewhere in the marketplace. I have focused on individuals with similar years of experience, educational backgrounds, and technical certifications. I have also reviewed several highly regarded annual salary guides and surveys that provide salary data by role, industry, and geography. That research consistently indicates that my base salary is well below the market average. I also continue to overachieve on my performance targets and have done so on a consistent basis for the past three years. Given the legitimate market data I referenced, which I have copied for our discussion today, I am seeking a base salary increase of 10% or $10,000.

Boss: That is too substantial of an increase. I am authorized and can agree to give you $4,000.

Employee: How about $7,000?

Boss: I can't agree to a penny over $5,000.

Employee: What if we split the difference?

Boss: We are $2,000 apart, so that would be $6,000.

Employee: OK. Let's agree on a $6,000 increase.

Boss: OK. $6,000 it is.

Even though this may seem like a reasonable result, it has created nothing but waste because it left both sides unhappy and dissatisfied. Did the parties even bother to discuss their interests or the range of satisfying options? Too often people want to "split the difference," and too often they leave plenty of waste on the table and end up feeling like the children in the story of Jack and Jill arguing over an orange. In that story, Jack and Jill are fighting over the last orange in the bowl. After they agree to split the orange in half, Jack takes his half, eats the fruit, and throws away the peel. Jill takes her half, throws away the fruit, and uses the peel to bake a cake. If Jack and Jill had simply discussed their interests, they would have used the entire orange. Instead, Jack's stomach is empty, and Jill's cake is flavorless. When you are in the boss's office and there is a disagreement over the amount of the raise, don't ever split oranges.

Figure 2 shows traditional bargaining that results in a compromise.

FIGURE 2

CLASSIC TRADITIONAL BARGAINING

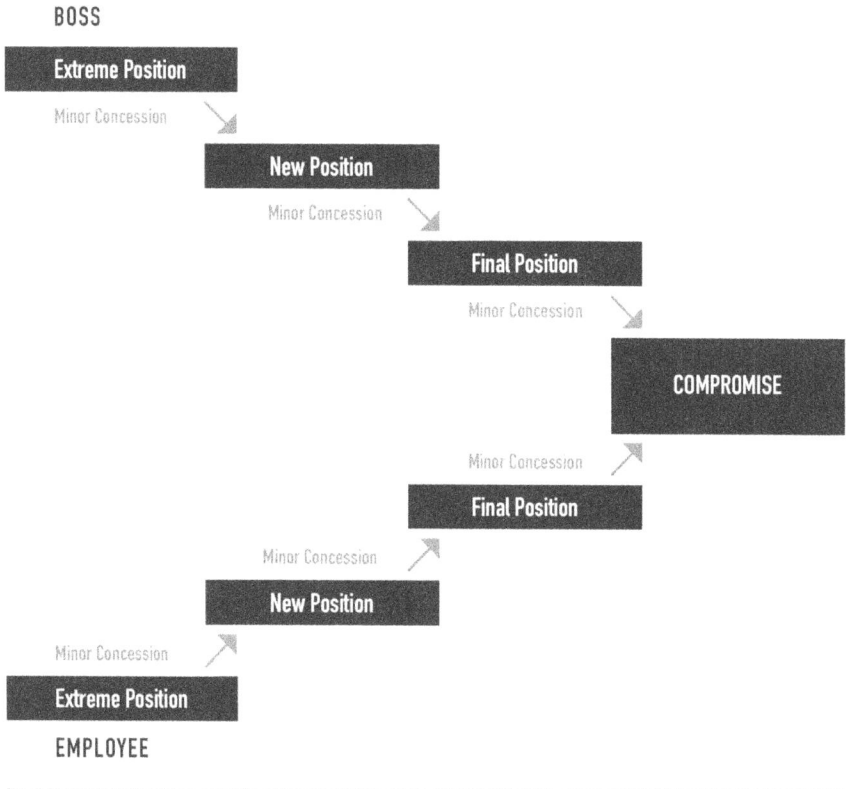

BOSS

Extreme Position

Minor Concession

New Position

Minor Concession

Final Position

Minor Concession

COMPROMISE

Minor Concession

Final Position

Minor Concession

New Position

Minor Concession

Extreme Position

EMPLOYEE

Let's now focus on an oldie but goodie: caving in. Caving in happens when one party to the negotiation firmly holds on to a position during the negotiation. Based upon the passage of time, the investment of resources, or some other event, that same party magically decides to give up that position and agree to the other party's demand. I find caving in to be one of the most frustrating things that a party to a negotiation can do. In that same vein, I have no patience for negotiators who aggressively assert their "bottom line," only to deviate from that number seconds later. If new terms are introduced, then I can accept the fact that you may need to reevaluate your bottom line.

Absent that scenario, your bottom line should truly be your bottom line, which is the last option you will accept before you go to your BATNA. So please refrain from using the term "bottom line" unless you mean it.

Why bother holding on to a position when you intended to give in all along? Holding on to that position yielded nothing but wasted time and effort for both parties. Caving in is not a page in the Rebel Negotiator's playbook. If a position is important on Day 1 of the negotiation, it will be just as important on Day 30 or Day 300. Rebel Negotiators say what they mean and mean what they say. They will not waste a bunch of time trying to get the other party to search for options to meet their interests, only to say "it's OK … just kidding" at the last minute.

Even though our negotiation with our boss may not last for 300 days, let's take a look at what caving in sounds like in the getting a raise context.

Employee: I have done a lot of market research regarding my current compensation level. I have looked at positions similar to mine at many of our key competitors and elsewhere in the marketplace. I have focused on individuals with similar years of experience, educational backgrounds, and technical certifications. I have also reviewed several highly regarded annual salary guides and surveys that provide salary data by role, industry, and geography. The research consistently indicates that my base salary is well below the market average. I also continue to overachieve on my performance targets and have done so on a consistent basis for the past three years. Given the legitimate market data I referenced, which I have copied for our discussion today, I am seeking a base salary increase of 10% or $10,000.

Boss: That seems quite a significant raise. I can agree to give you a $5,000 salary increase.

Employee: I have done my research and $10,000 is a legitimate and market-relevant raise given my years of experience, tenure, capabilities, and performance. I simply will not accept a penny less.

This is my bottom line and a *deal breaker* for me.

Boss: An increase of that size will require me to escalate to my boss and to Human Resources. Let me talk with them and see what I can do for you.

Employee: OK, but to be clear, I will not accept anything less than $10,000

A week passes by…

Boss: I spoke with my boss and the best we can do is $7,500. I am even going to give everyone else on the team a smaller increase to accommodate this request.

Employee: I appreciate that and understand the impact this will have on the team, but I simply can't agree to anything less than $10,000.

Two weeks pass, and the conversation resumes.

Boss: OK. I have done everything I can. I called the general manager of our region and even went directly to the CEO to advocate on your behalf. The best increase we can offer is $7,500. Is that acceptable?

Employee: OK. I will agree to $7,500.

Boss: If you were willing to accept $7,500, then why didn't you just accept that offer two weeks ago? I have been working on options with Human Resources and Finance to get you the $10,000 increase for two weeks given you told me it was your bottom line. I went directly to the CEO, and now my integrity has been undermined. I really wish you had remained principled and disciplined and told me you were going to your BATNA. If you had done so, I was authorized to give you the $10,000 increase.

As you can see, this is an extremely frustrating set of circumstances. Why did you finally say "yes" after all this time of saying "no"? You should put your best foot forward in the negotiation. If $7,500 was an acceptable offer that satisfies your interests, then please just accept the offer. In this case, the offer could have been accepted much earlier in this process, and the deal could have been finalized with plenty of time left over for dinner and a bottle of wine. By continuing to say "no," you have done nothing but waste time and undermine the negotiation. Think about how the boss will react the next time you come in seeking a raise or anything else for that matter and tell her your bottom line. Do you think she will take you seriously and respond in a principled and disciplined manner? *Figure 3 shows caving in.*

FIGURE 3

CAVING IN

BOSS

| Extreme Position | → | Extreme Position | → | COMPROMISE |

GIVE UP POSITION

| Extreme Position | → | Extreme Position |

EMPLOYEE

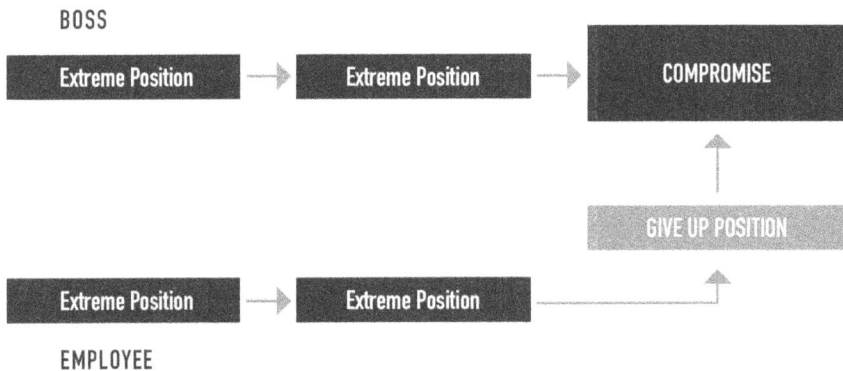

Now, let's play chicken. This game typically involves two vehicles driven directly toward each other to test which driver will swerve away first. In the context of negotiation, playing chicken means the parties make mutual challenges or threats, hoping the other party will withdraw or acquiesce before a conflict or a collision occurs. Usually, this game reaches an impasse, forcing the parties to pursue an alternative. My advice is this: Never play chicken with your boss. The stakes are simply too high. You might lose the game and your job. Given the legitimacy of your request for a raise and the strength of your BATNA, there is no need to play such a dangerous game.

Let's take a look at what playing chicken sounds like in the getting a raise context.

Employee: I have done a lot of market research regarding my current compensation level. I have looked at positions similar to mine at many of our key competitors and elsewhere in the marketplace. I have focused on individuals with similar years of experience, educational backgrounds, and technical certifications. I have also reviewed several highly regarded annual salary guides and surveys that provide salary data by role, industry, and geography. The research consistently indicates that my base salary is well below the market average. I also continue to overachieve on my performance targets and have done so on a consistent basis for the past three years. Given the legitimate market data I referenced, which I have copied for our discussion today, I am seeking a base salary increase of 10% or $10,000.

Boss: That is simply not possible. The most I will agree to is a $3,000 salary increase.

Employee: $10,000 is what I want. I have done my research and $10,000 is a legitimate and market-relevant raise given my years of experience, tenure, capabilities, and performance.

Boss: I will not agree to $10,000. I will agree to a $3,500 increase.

Employee: I will agree to a $9,000 increase but no less.

Boss: Maybe I wasn't clear. I will not agree to anything even close to $10,000. My final offer is $4,000.

Employee: Well maybe I wasn't clear regarding the legitimacy of my request. To move this forward, I will agree to an $8,500 increase and that is my bottom line.

Boss: My final offer really is $4,000. I am not joking.

Employee: I am not joking either. When I said my bottom line was $8,500, I meant it.

Boss: Are you going to accept my final offer of $4,000?

Employee: I do not accept your offer. Are you going to accept my offer of $8,500?

Boss: I will not, and I don't have too much time to discuss this matter further.

Employee: So that's it. You are not going to budge? You are really going to let me leave over a few thousand dollars?

Boss: I am not going to budge a penny. You can leave anytime you want. Are you sure you don't want the $4,000?

Employee: I will pass on the $4,000 and will be leaving early this afternoon because I have a job interview.

Boss: You can leave now. That will give me time to call Human Resources and post the job opening before my next meeting.

Figure 4 shows a game of chicken.

FIGURE 4

LET'S PLAY CHICKEN

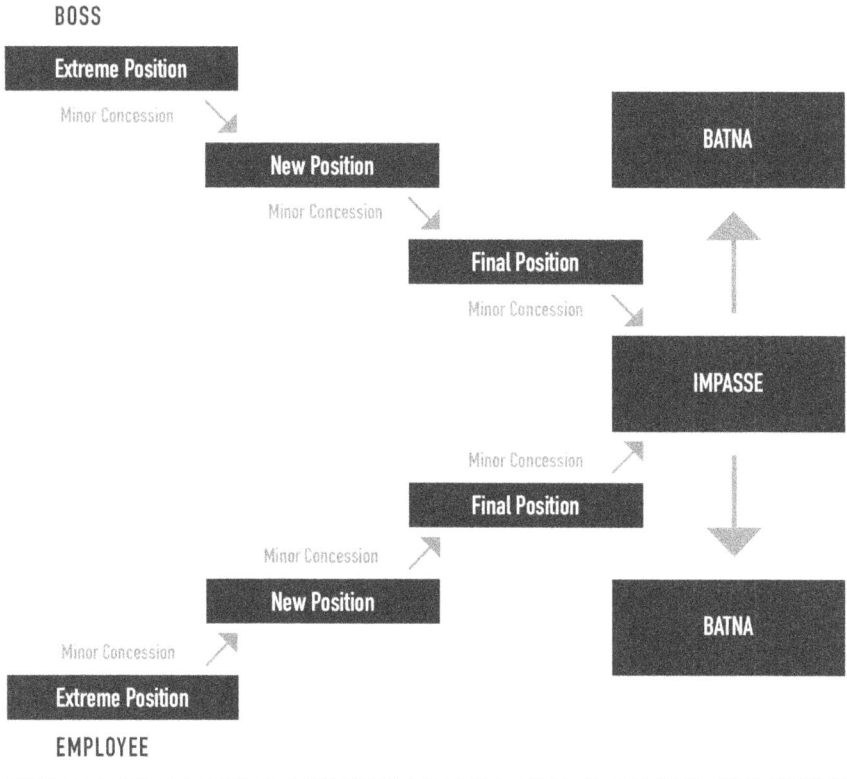

So, you won't be playing chicken, but let's also make sure that anchoring will not be rewarded. Anchoring happens when the opposing party sticks to its position while you provide offer after offer to move toward that position. Let's see what that sounds like when you are trying to get a much-deserved raise.

Employee: I have done a lot of market research regarding my current compensation level. I have looked at positions like mine at many of our key competitors and elsewhere in the marketplace. I have focused on individuals with similar years of experience, educational backgrounds, and technical certifications. I have also reviewed several highly regarded annual salary guides and surveys that provide salary data by role, industry, and geography. The research consistently indicates that my base salary is well below the market average. I also continue to overachieve on my performance targets and have done so on a consistent basis for the past three years. Given the legitimate market data I referenced, which I have copied for our discussion today, I am seeking a base salary increase of 10% or $10,000.

Boss: You know how much I value you as a member of my team but the most I can offer is $5,000. That really is the best I can do given budgetary constraints.

Employee: OK. How about $8,000?

Boss: No, really the best I can do is $5,000. I can't approve an increase for more than 5%.

Employee: OK. I will come down to $6,000, but that is my bottom line.

Boss: I appreciate the fact that you are trying to be flexible in this process, but I simply can't do any better than $5,000.

Employee: I understand your position, but if you truly value me as a member of your team, then please work with me a little bit. My best and really final offer is $5,500. Come on. Work with me a little bit. What's $500 between friends?

Boss: I have an idea. Let's split the difference and agree on $5,250. I am going to get in trouble with Human Resources, but I will deal with that for you.

Employee: OK. I really appreciate it. You have a deal. I am going to get back to work now.

In this scenario, not only did the employee reward his boss for anchoring to the initial $5,000 offer, but he added insult to injury by agreeing to split the difference. Ultimately, the boss agreed to a minor $250 concession, whereas the employee reduced his original demand and market-relevant salary increase by around 47 percent. We will not reward our bosses for anchoring to salary increases that are not grounded in legitimacy. Here, you should express your extreme dissatisfaction to your boss and fine-tune your resume. *Figure 5 shows a game of rewarding anchoring.*

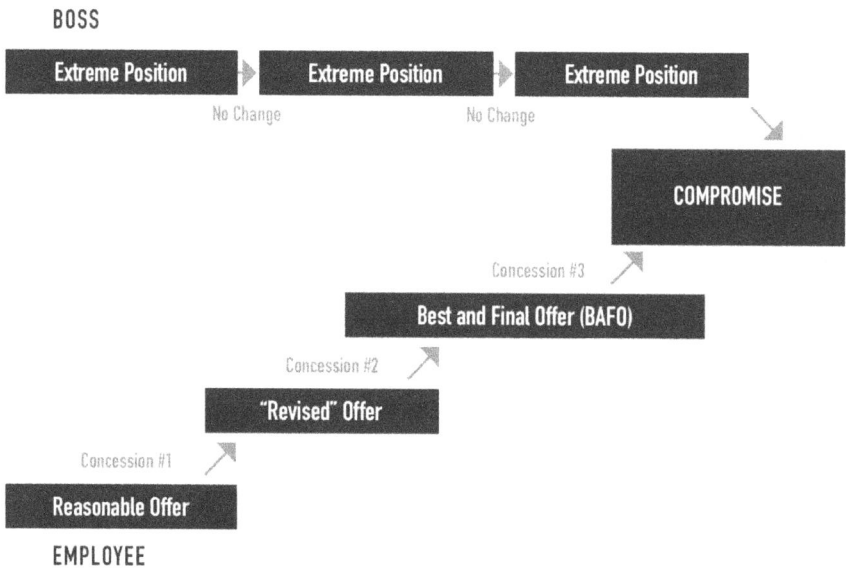

FIGURE 5

REWARDING ANCHORING

BOSS

| Extreme Position | → | Extreme Position | → | Extreme Position |

No Change   No Change

COMPROMISE

Concession #3

Best and Final Offer (BAFO)

Concession #2

"Revised" Offer

Concession #1

Reasonable Offer

EMPLOYEE

The last game I want you to spot is entrapment. From the second you enter your boss's office, remember you are free to say no and not compelled to accept an offer that is illegitimate and sub-optimal. You are not detained, restrained, or kept in custody. Before you sit down and begin the negotiation, make a mental note of all the exits and be prepared to use them if you must. Also, check your clothing and the chair you're sitting in, and make sure there's no Velcro.

Entrapment occurs when you enter the boss's office and you really need to get a salary increase. You are desperate and while $10,000 is 100% legitimate, you will acquiesce and accept something less. Maybe you don't have another job lined up and feel like an indentured servant. Maybe you need some increase, even if immaterial, just to make you feel better. Maybe you can't stand negotiation and simply want the process to end. In each scenario, you are overwhelmed by the belief that you can't walk away because you have nowhere to walk to.

As I told you in *The Rebel Negotiator's Guide to Buying a Car*, you will never have a stronger BATNA in your life than when you enter a car dealership to purchase a new car—period. I don't care if you like the dealership, like the salesperson, love the car, like the free Otis Spunkmeyer cookies, or whatever your excuse.

Negotiating with your boss is significantly different than negotiating with the car salesperson. It is not so easy to get up and leave the building on principle if you don't get the raise you are seeking. That doesn't mean you can't be disciplined and principled in your approach and remain mindful of the BATNA strength of both parties. Assuming you are a high performing employee, you likely have a strong alternative as you would be appealing to other employers. Always remember that replacing employees at all hierarchical levels comes at a cost both in terms of hiring a replacement as well as the impact from institutional knowledge leaving the building.

My mom has always told me it is a lot easier to look for and secure a new job while you have a job, and, on this issue, she is spot-on in her assessment. I am not suggesting you need to threaten to leave your current employer or actually do so if they do not meet your expectations when it comes to a raise. What I am suggesting is that it is always a good idea to have a BATNA you can execute against if necessary. Knowing you have a BATNA will make you feel confident in your negotiation approach, will keep you principled and disciplined and focused on legitimacy at the table, and will keep you from folding like a lawn chair when faced with threats or push-back from your boss.

Now that you can spot the game, I'd like to discuss the importance of mental awareness when you're seated at the negotiation table. Ultimately, your level of success at the table and your method of engaging with others will be shaped by your social style, your personality type, and how you deal with conflict. No matter what, it is important to be a good listener, to inquire instead of advocate, to seek to understand instead of seeking to be understood, and to find the right balance between directness and diplomacy. Finally, before you sit at the negotiation table, ask yourself if you want to be right or to be effective. When it comes to negotiating with your boss, the answer to this question will require some extensive thought.

As you seek to understand, make an effort to leave any bias you have at the door. In a negotiation context, bias is defined as a refusal to consider the possible merits of alternative points of view. Bias will poison a negotiation if you view your side as better, more legitimate, and more honest while undermining the perspective of the other party. Suggesting that the ideas of the other party are extreme or stubborn will likely exaggerate your perception of their position and the actual amount of conflict that exists between the parties. Ultimately, this can impact the ability of the parties to reach an agreement. Remember: Bias kills a negotiation. To keep bias in check, don't get too committed to your point of view, slow down, listen, and inquire.

One key component that will affect your ability to be a successful negotiator is how you approach conflict. The Thomas-Kilmann Conflict Mode Instrument is a popular tool that assesses a person's behavior in conflict situations, in which the concerns of people appear to be incompatible. The instrument measures two factors: (1) assertiveness, the extent that the person attempts to satisfy the person's own concerns; and (2) cooperativeness, the extent that the person attempts to satisfy the other person's concerns. Ultimately, these behaviors can define five methods of dealing with conflict: competing, collaborating, compromising, avoiding, and accommodating. *Figure 6 shows the types of conflict modes measured against the assertiveness and cooperativeness scales.* Let me describe each method in more detail:

FIGURE 6

THOMAS-KILMANN CONFLICT MODE INSTRUMENT

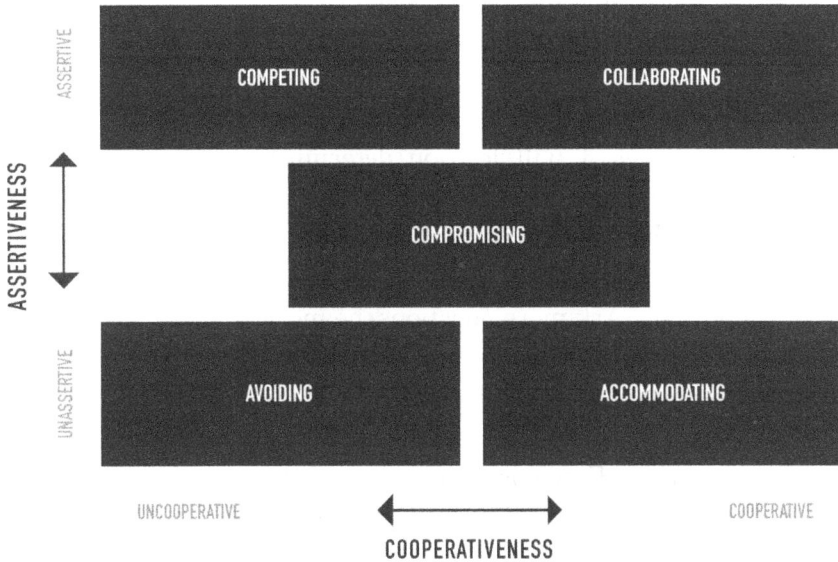

1. **Competitor:** A competitor is both assertive and uncooperative and pursues his own interests at the expense of others. A competitor wants to win and will use whatever means are at his disposal to do so.

2. **Collaborator:** A collaborator is both assertive and cooperative. A collaborator attempts to find a solution that satisfies the interests of both parties.

3. **Compromiser:** A compromiser is midway between both assertiveness and cooperativeness. The compromiser tries to find an acceptable solution that partially satisfies the interests of both parties. As I previously discussed, compromisers like to split oranges.

4. **Avoider:** An avoider is both unassertive and uncooperative

and, as the name indicates, avoids conflict completely.

5. **Accommodator:** An accommodator is the opposite of the competitor in that he neglects his own concerns to satisfy the concerns of the other party.

No one conflict-handling mode is best because each may be used depending on the circumstances. I will let you determine your social style, your personality type, and your style of approaching conflict, but I will give you high-level advice that you can use if your profile is strong in any one area.

1. **Competitor:** Ask more questions, be more flexible, decide if the relationship matters, and don't be overly confident in the strength of your alternative.

2. **Collaborator:** Focus on preparation, and take the time to clearly understand the interests of both parties.

3. **Compromiser:** Don't split oranges. Don't accept the first acceptable answer, and be more creative.

4. **Avoider:** Get help if necessary. Conflict is not a bad thing. You can disagree without being disagreeable.

5. **Accommodator:** Be more active in the negotiation. Don't be afraid to assert your interests, and focus on objective criteria that support the reasonableness of those interests. Don't underestimate the strength of your alternative.

Even if your social style and personality type are so heavily ingrained in who you are that they cannot change, you can successfully temper your approach to conflict at the negotiation table. I speak from experience as an extremely competitive person: I've learned to temper my approach to conflict by keeping my competitive arousal in check and focusing on collaboration, so I can be more effective at the negotiation table.

You will be competing at the highest level when you negotiate to secure a raise, and the stakes are high. You will focus on your interests but also be mindful of the interests of your boss and ultimately your employer. With that said, you will use whatever means necessary to get the best possible raise you can. If you are able to find an option that meets your interests, then you will proceed to an agreement. If not, then you may need to assert or execute your BATNA. As you navigate through the process, you will be self-aware, keep your competitive arousal in check, and focus on your goal: seeing those extra Benjamins flow into your bank account on payday.

As for self-awareness, it is important to find an appropriate balance between focusing on your interests at the expense of other party and winning at all costs. In their May 2008 *Harvard Business Review* article, "When Winning Is Everything," Deepak Malhotra, Gillian Ku, and J. Keith Murnighan suggested that the win-at-all-costs type of decision-making was driven by an "adrenaline-fueled emotional state," called competitive arousal. You can probably think of a time when you were a victim of competitive arousal and made a decision in the heat of battle that, in retrospect, looked foolish. Sometimes, you want to win at all costs, even if the decision-making process lacks sound judgment and is solely based on competitive arousal. To mitigate this win-at-all-costs dynamic, it is crucial that you stay disciplined at the negotiation table, keep in mind your ultimate goal, and manage your emotions. By taking this approach, you can keep your competitive arousal in check, and you can secure your ultimate objective of being paid a market-relevant and legitimate salary.

MAINTAIN DISCIPLINE AND FOLLOW THE PROCESS

To be a successful negotiator, you must have a strict methodology that you use in every negotiation. That methodology is the third key ingredient in your recipe for becoming a successful negotiator after influence and mental and situational awareness. The first step is to identify your goal for the negotiation. If you don't know your goal, then you might as well call it a day and play golf. Once you have identified your goal, the next step is preparation. I strictly follow the approach that former New York Giants head Coach Tom Coughlin shared during a press conference before Super Bowl XLVI, "humble enough to prepare, confident enough to perform."

As you prepare, remember that the negotiation may not flow as smoothly as it did when you role-played in the mirror or with your friends, family, or office colleagues. In the words of the great philosopher and pugilist Mike Tyson: "Everyone has a plan till they get punched in the mouth." As long as you can spot the game and use the methodology I will discuss, the punch should leave you unfazed and ready for more action.

Let's assume you have reined in your competitive arousal, you clearly know your goal, you have prepared diligently, and you are about to begin negotiating. The key question is: How do you reach an agreement that meets your interests and is acceptable to your boss and your employer? My answer has been the same for many years and has served me well in the marketplace: 4x7. This approach has four key principles and seven elements, and, frankly, is easy to understand. If you can master 4x7, then you are well on your way to becoming a very successful negotiator. These are the four principles:

1. **Temper your approach based upon the amount of risk in the outcome.** How critical is securing the salary increase? Do you have financial or other commitments upon which it is predicated? If you don't get the increase you are seeking, can you legitimately pursue your alternative? Have you already secured another job offer? Can you afford to be out of work while you are job hunting? Will you accept a smaller increase this year with a commitment to conduct a mid-year salary review? Will you accept some other form of compensation in lieu of a base salary increase—a bonus tied to the achievement of a series of objective, measurable, and verifiable performance targets, additional paid time off, the ability to work a modified or flexible schedule, or possibly tuition reimbursement for a degree you have been pursuing?

2. **Temper your approach based on the relevant geography.** The way you approach the boss in New York may be different from the way you approach the boss in Omaha.

3. **Temper your approach based upon the person sitting across from you at the negotiation table.** Be mindful of the personality type and social style of your boss, and engage with her accordingly. Think about how your boss approaches conflict and fine-tune your negotiation strategy accordingly.

4. **Remember that conflicts are created, conducted, and sustained by human beings and can be resolved by human beings.** Yes, it is a raise and is important, but there

is no need to get overly stressed or anxious. You have to feel confident in the legitimacy of your request. Take a deep breath, remain calm, slow down, listen carefully, be firm in your interests but flexible regarding options by which they are met, and be ready to assert or execute your BATNA if necessary.

Principle 4 is a recent addition to the list—a list I had not changed in over 15 years. The addition came from a 2010 speech by former U.S. Senate Majority Leader George Mitchell, who had just been named as a special envoy to the Middle East, a very critical and challenging role. After being introduced at the appointment ceremony, Mitchell said: "Conflicts are created, conducted, and sustained by human beings, and can be resolved by human beings." I am in no way comparing obtaining an annual salary increase to negotiating peace in the Middle East, but you should keep the scope of the negotiation in perspective throughout the process.

The 4x7's seven-element approach in a principled negotiation stems from the book *Getting to Yes*, by Roger Fisher and William Ury of the Harvard Negotiation Project. The seven elements are interests, options, legitimacy, alternatives, commitment, communication, and relationship. The key to success is your ability to identify these elements and how they connect, and most importantly, to understand how they evolve during a negotiation. As I previously discussed, it is also critical that you take the time to prepare for any negotiation and carefully consider how the seven elements can affect it. If you have not prepared properly, you might as well cancel the meeting because the result will not be good. Remember Coach Coughlin's approach: "humble enough to prepare, confident enough to perform." I say: "Learn it, know it, and live it."

While I am quoting people, take a look at what Harvey Specter, the lawyer in the television show *Suits*, said: "What are your choices when someone puts a gun to your head? …What are you talking about? You do what they say or they shoot you. WRONG. You take the gun, or you pull out a bigger one. Or, you call their bluff. Or, you do one of a hundred and forty-six other things." Remember that your BATNA is not weak—assuming that you are a high performer—when negotiating for a raise.

Ultimately, these seven elements will dictate your likelihood of success in any negotiation. How these elements are interconnected is demonstrated in the negotiation, the desired goal of which is reaching an agreement that satisfies the mutual interests of the parties. If an option is identified that meets those interests, then there is a clear path forward; if not, then the parties may have to pursue their alternatives, also known—as I have previously mentioned—as their best alternative to a negotiated agreement (BATNA). As I like to say, negotiation is that simple and that complex. Let's revisit those seven elements, in more detail:

1. **Interests:** What are the needs, concerns, goals, hopes, and fears that are motivating the other party to negotiate?

2. **Options:** What approaches can be identified that meet the mutual interests of the parties?

3. **Legitimacy:** What criteria exist—industry practices, expert opinions, laws, rules or regulations, or precedent— to measure if the options considered or agreement reached is fair and sensible?

4. **Alternatives:** What unilateral steps can either party take—how can their interests be satisfied elsewhere— if the parties can't reach an agreement?

5. **Commitment:** Is the other party prepared to reach an agreement and does the party have the power to do it?

6. **Communication:** Are the parties collaborating by listening and talking to each other, and remaining unconditionally constructive?

7. **Relationship:** Do I care about maintaining a relationship with the party across the table?

The focus on and the benchmark for success should be an agreement that:

- Satisfies the interests of the parties

- Minimizes waste and reflects the best of many options

- Makes neither party feel taken advantage of by the option chosen

- Is better than your best alternative, or BATNA

- Embodies a commitment among the parties

- Is grounded in open communication

- Reinforces the relationship between the parties

Your ability to spot the seven elements will very much help you execute an agreement. *Figure 7 shows an overall view of the seven elements.*

FIGURE 7

THE SEVEN ELEMENTS

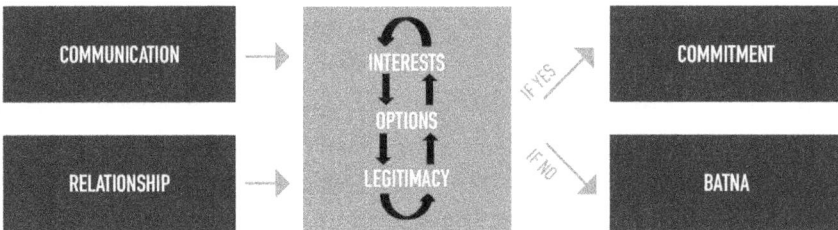

You can read lots of books and attend plenty of trainings on successful negotiation techniques and tactics. However, I assure you that if you strictly follow the four core principles and keep a laser focus on the seven elements, you will make great strides in the art of negotiation.

Lets review the other principles at the core of negotiation. What does it mean to temper your negotiation approach based upon the amount of risk in the outcome? As I previously discussed, you should consider a variety of factors in measuring such risk. Risk factors that impact the outcome may include the criticality of securing the salary increase, the existence of any financial or other commitments upon which it is predicated, the ability to legitimately—financially or personally—pursue your alternative, and the likelihood of securing other employment in a timely manner. Other factors would include your openness to accepting a smaller increase now with the agreement to conduct a mid-year review; agreeing to some other form of compensation in lieu of a base salary increase, likely a bonus tied to the achievement of a series of objective, measurable, and verifiable performance targets; additional paid time off; the ability to work a modified or flexible schedule; or possibly tuition reimbursement for a degree you have been pursuing. What will the impact of these decisions be on your performance, your finances, and, most of all, your happiness?

According to the second principle, it is important to temper your approach based upon your geographic region. What works well in New York or San Francisco might not work well in New Orleans or Dallas. Before jumping into the negotiation, you must understand the effect that culture may have on the negotiation. Is the style of your company or your counterpart quiet and less flamboyant, requiring some level of deference, or louder and more aggressive? I will tell you: Prepare and temper your approach accordingly.

Finally, remember to temper your style and approach based upon the person sitting across from you at the negotiation table. Although you can study countless books on negotiation tactics, I urge you to make every attempt to understand the style, personality, motivation, emotions, and interests of the person with whom you will be negotiating. Ultimately, your success hinges on your ability to work with that person to reach an agreement with an acceptable level of risk and reward for the parties to the transaction.

I would like to introduce you to the "Harley Principle." I have been riding Harley-Davidson motorcycles for the past 18 years, and it is a great passion of mine. I have a V-Rod and a Screamin' Eagle Springer, and I love the feeling of rolling down the road with the wind in my face on a beautiful summer day. If I enter the office of the person I will be negotiating with and see anything Harley-Davidson or motorcycle related, I always ask about it, and the conversation quickly shifts to a passion we both share. Now it is likely you have already established a strong level of affiliation with your boss and hopefully share some common interests. I urge you to utilize that level of affiliation to your advantage when engaging in the salary discussion. Don't overplay it, but remember that the relationship may be just as important to her as it is to you.

Finding this common interest allows you to identify with each other in a way that transcends the substance of the negotiation and the potentially adversarial negotiations that you are about to undertake. Although I am not suggesting that a common passion for Harley-Davidson motorcycles results in an easy negotiation, it allows me to identify with the person I'm dealing with. Even though I have no scientific evidence, I can absolutely tell you that my negotiations with motorcycle enthusiasts over the years have been very successful. So, try to identify with the party you'll be negotiating with; it will definitely make a difference.

THIS IS NOT GOING TO BE PLEASANT

The final ingredient in the recipe for becoming a successful negotiator is the ability to have a difficult conversation. As we all know, negotiations are not always focused on rainbows and lollipops, and as President John F. Kennedy said: "Let us never negotiate out of fear. But let us never fear to negotiate." You must be ready, willing, and able to engage in a difficult conversation.

Your comfort level in doing this will be tightly connected to how you approach conflict. Competitors will be ready to jump right in as they want to win at all costs. For avoiders, having a difficult conversation is like having a root canal.

Sometimes the difficult conversation causes stress and anxiety because you have a relationship with the other party. Delivering a difficult message to a party with whom you want to maintain a relationship is much more challenging than one where the level of engagement is business only, at best. The conversation with your boss is a challenging one as you want to maintain a good working relationship with her but at the same time don't want the relationship to unduly impact the principled, disciplined, and legitimate decision-making process you will strictly adhere to during the negotiation. Depending upon how the negotiation unfolds, you may need to prepare yourself to deliver some difficult messages that could include, "I am going to leave if I don't get the increase I want," or "I don't want to have our relationship impact the substance of these discussions."

To build a level of comfort for a difficult conversation, I recommend that you take these four key steps:

1. **Be prepared.** Preparation is an absolute necessity for any negotiation and even more so for delivering a difficult message. I can't stress enough the importance of thorough preparation. Remember the old saying: If you fail to prepare, then prepare to fail. Make sure that you have an in-depth understanding of the issues and that you focus on legitimacy. If necessary, you can role-play the negotiation with a friend or colleague.

2. **Seek to understand instead of seeking to be understood.** The difference may seem subtle, but it is significant and will affect the tone and tenor of your conversation. Use inquiry instead of advocacy and find the right balance between diplomacy and directness.

3. **Prepare yourself for a negative reaction.** The conversation may become tense. Your preparation should help you become emotionally ready. Keep your competitive arousal in check—ask yourself, do you want to be right or to be effective?

4. **Keep things in perspective.** How significant is the message and the issue? Will it even matter in six months? In six years?

THE SEVEN ELEMENTS IN ACTION

Now that you have the recipe for becoming a successful negotiator, let's think about how you can perfect it for your salary discussion. I will conduct an in-depth analysis of each of the seven elements, but let's first look at the overall approach.

When you sit down at the negotiating table, your ultimate objective should be to strive for an effective and efficient negotiation. To be effective, you should communicate in an open, honest, and candid manner with the other party. To do this, I strongly urge you to focus on your ability to listen carefully. A good acronym to remember to help you do this is to be a good **LIAR**— **(L)**isten, **(I)**nquire, **(A)**cknowledge, and **(R)**espond. I encourage you to seek to understand instead of seeking to be understood, and use inquiry instead of advocacy. Do not talk past each other. It is amazing how much you can learn by slowing down, listening, and asking questions. The other element of an effective negotiation is to maintain a good working relationship with the other party. For the competitors out there, I recommend that you establish a level of affiliation—even if it is at a basic and superficial level—with your counterpart. By doing this, you will see that person in a more human light and be more inclined to collaborate. I will assume you have some level of affiliation with your boss, but if you don't, focus on cultivating some level of affiliation going forward. Doing so might facilitate a more collaborative and comfortable discussion, especially one focused on a difficult topic such as getting a raise.

For efficiency, I strive for a negotiation that will allow me to make the best and most informed decision; I will not accept a bad result because I am either emotional or anchored to my position. To help you make the best and most informed decision possible, the seven-element model focuses on the relevant interests of the parties. You must be cognizant of the interests of both parties. Then you can develop options, one of which will, hopefully, satisfy those interests and allow the parties to reach an agreement and make a commitment. The hope is that the mutually acceptable option is grounded in legitimacy—it is fair and reasonable and has been tested against market standards—and is better than each party's alternative.

I urge you to take as much time as necessary to think carefully about the full range of options that may satisfy the interests of the parties. When you think you have exhausted the potential options, think again. Be open to considering all options; rather than saying no, think about under what conditions you might say yes.

Your intent once you cross the threshold of your boss's office is to engage in an effective and efficient negotiation. It will be successful if you negotiate in a way that achieves these goals:

- Satisfies the interests of the parties and does not create waste

- Results in the best of many options

- Grounded in legitimacy and fairness

- Better than your best alternative

- Memorialized in a well-planned commitment

- Built on a foundation of good communication

- Follows a process that improves the working relationship

Now that you have a basic understanding of the seven-element process, I will thoroughly review each element and how it will affect your salary discussion.

RELATIONSHIP—CAN'T WE ALL JUST GET ALONG?

If I were giving you general advice in the spirit of achieving an effective negotiation, I would strongly recommend that you build a good working relationship with the other party you're negotiating with. My advice would apply even if the interaction is purely transactional. As you can likely ascertain, the Rebel Negotiator does not avoid conflict; his Thomas-Kilmann compete score is off the chart. That approach has earned him another nickname: Bulldog.

But there are times when the Bulldog must stay in his cage to be effective. A key component of being a successful negotiator is to find a way to humanize the adversarial process by establishing an affiliation with the person you are negotiating with. Then you will be able to see your adversary in a more human light, and your desire to collaborate with that person should increase. Even if such affiliation is, at best, only superficial, it is an extremely important part of the negotiation. When it comes to negotiating with your boss, I want you to be mindful of your goal—finding an option that meets your interests but doing so in a collaborative manner.

Unlike going into a car dealership where the last thing on your list of priorities is building a relationship, the rules are a bit different when negotiating with your boss. The way in which you engage may depend upon the relative BATNA strength of the parties, but I would suggest you engage in a collaborative manner even if your boss has a weak BATNA. Why shouldn't you take advantage of her given the relative balance of power in this negotiation? The answer is simple and two-fold: (1) you might get your salary increase but your boss may make your life miserable for the foreseeable future; and (2) well, you know what they say about payback. So even if your BATNA is strong, remain principled and disciplined, be firm in your interests, but flexible in terms of options to meet those interests. This approach should let you win the battle but not lose the war.

For those of you who like to compete and relish the idea of negotiating with your boss when she has a weak BATNA, I would ask you to think carefully about the following questions:

1. How often do you rely on your boss for a salary increase, for a performance review, for a promotion, or for something else? Do you think it will matter in six months, one, two, or three years, what, if any, relationship you build with her?

2. What is the probability your boss will still be serving in that capacity when it is time for the next performance and salary review?

3. For those instances where a policy exception is required, how influential can your boss be in securing the exception? Will your relationship help her go the extra mile for you?

4. Has maintaining a good working relationship with your boss served you well over time?

5. If you take advantage of your boss when she has a weak BATNA, will she do the same when the table is turned?

As you have seen in the situational awareness scenarios we previously reviewed, a common tactic that your boss may deploy is to use a policy, budgetary constraint, or financial performance as the reason why the raise you are seeking is not legitimate or attainable. She may also assert that approving such an increase is beyond her authority.

This tactic is similar to what you may encounter when negotiating with the car salesman. To the extent he can't give you the price or term you want, he will just blame the sales manager. In the car dealership, this challenge can be easily addressed. Because we could possibly care less about maintaining a relationship with the car salesperson, we simply go around him and ask to negotiate directly with the sales manager of the dealership.

Escalating the matter can be a little more delicate when negotiating with your boss. While you want to be respectful of her role and authority, the negotiation can quickly come to a halt if she simply tells you that the amount of salary increase you are seeking is not something that she can approve, that it conflicts with a policy or other budgetary directive she was given, or that the timing is not right given some financial or other performance issue. All these tactics sound as if she simply wants to avoid having a difficult conversation that is grounded in legitimacy. While policies and procedures may be legitimate, they are not sheathing behind which your boss can hide when it comes to your salary increase.

While you want to respect your boss, it is not legitimate to simply accept that answer as final, accept a sub-optimal salary increase that is not legitimate or consistent with the research you have conducted, and call it a day. You can ask your boss who is authorized to make an exception to the policy or who has the approval authority for the increase you are seeking. Request that your boss include that person in the discussion or facilitate a meeting between you and that person directly. Alternatively, ask your boss to go advocate on your behalf. If this approach is not successful, you may have to go to your alternative, and go around your boss to obtain the relief you are seeking.

While I realize this is dangerous territory, your options are limited: you can either die at her hand or go around her to the person with the authority to approve.

The bottom line is I strongly suggest you build a strong relationship with the party with whom you will be negotiating. With that said, please remember to separate that relationship from the substance of the negotiation.

COMMUNICATION—
I'M SORRY, I DON'T UNDERSTAND YOU

Irrespective of the extent of the relationship you have or intend to cultivate with the other party to the negotiation, it is important you can communicate with him in a clear, concise, and efficient manner. I can't stress enough the importance of listening to the other party and seeking to understand instead of seeking to be understood. So often in a negotiation, the parties find themselves talking past each other and hear only their position, and not the interests behind it. Disciplined negotiators listen for the interests behind those positions and the standards the other party is using to support his perspective. At a basic level, negotiation is a task of influence. In order to influence the other party, I need to understand the party's interests as deeply as possible, so I can generate options that will address those interests and, hopefully, lead to a better agreement.

I encourage a very direct and firm approach with your boss in the salary discussion—say what you mean and mean what you say. Prepare, prepare, and prepare again. Know the amount of increase you are seeking and some options by which it can be satisfied and know your bottom line. In terms of the exact amount or the acceptable price range, a colleague suggests not using round numbers. He believes that communicating an exact number, namely, "I want an increase of $10,425," is more effective and reflects significant diligence in preparing the offer. According to a 2019 study conducted by LeanIn.org and McKinsey & Co., those failing to ask for a specific amount in a salary negotiation received 32% less on average than the ones who did. Other than that statistic, I have no scientific evidence to support his claim, so I will leave this to your discretion.

When you go in to meet your boss, be clear on your demand. By this point in time, you will have conducted plenty of due diligence and will have prepared for the negotiation. Given the amount of time you prepared and the ample legitimacy upon which your increase is predicated, please have some confidence and conviction in your message.

All of your communication should be direct, firm, and unemotional. There is no crying in negotiation, at least not when you are negotiating a salary increase. Make sure and tell your boss your key interests and the parameters you require to reach an agreement. If she agrees or puts forth an option that meets your interests, then be ready, willing, and able to shake hands and get back to the rest of your day. If she does not agree, and you are unable to identify any options that will meet the interests of both parties, then be prepared to go to your BATNA.

HOW EXACTLY IS THIS GAME PLAYED?

Before I discuss interests and consider options, I will talk about some things to consider when preparing for the salary negotiation including how to perform the proper level of due diligence that will serve as legitimacy for your raise as well as how to prioritize your interests. It is important to carefully prioritize your interests in order to evaluate the various options that will be discussed during the negotiation. I will let you determine how best to prioritize your interests but have provided some thought-provoking questions to help you navigate through that process:

1. **Is an increase in salary what you really want?** Are there other things that might give you more satisfaction? Do you want to take on or be relieved of certain responsibilities? Do you want to have fewer direct reports? Do you want to report to someone different? Do you want to work from home two days a week? Do you want to have a more flexible schedule? Do you care about a title or the size of your office? Do you want a shorter commute? Do you want to work fewer hours? Remember that all of the above items can be translated into hard dollars or into personal happiness. When you contemplate the balance between a salary increase and other things that may result in greater

personal happiness, think carefully about the following James Patterson quote: "Imagine life is a game in which you are juggling five balls. The balls are called work, family, health, friends, and integrity. And you're keeping all of them in the air. But one day you finally come to understand that work is a rubber ball. If you drop it, it will bounce back. The other four balls are made of glass. If you drop one of these, it will be irrevocably scuffed, nicked, perhaps even shattered."

2. **Take the time to know your goal as you go into the negotiation.** Think about what you value and let that influence the outcome. If you only want the hard dollars and the answer is no, will you accept more vacation, training, or schedule flexibility? Is there any possibility to turn the no into a yes in six months?

3. **What is the time horizon in which you want to get your salary increase?** Should I think about simply getting more money in the current period or negotiating for the tools and capabilities I will need to be successful two or three years from now?

4. **Are you being realistic in terms of the increase you are seeking?** Have you conducted a salary benchmarking exercise in which you have compared yourself to similarly situated individuals serving in a similar role in a similar industry in a similarly sized organization and geographic market? You need to be honest with yourself as you go through this process. Can you point to specific results you have achieved in the prior performance period that can support the increase you are seeking? Do you have feedback from your peers or others which addresses the quality of the work you delivered and the corresponding impact it had on results? Take the time to build a rock-solid case that justifies a potential increase in salary. If your request

for a raise is not grounded in legitimacy it is simply a fool's errand.

5. **Are you doubting your value or accepting less than you are entitled?** The second that you begin to doubt your value to the organization you might as well call it a day and go play golf. Once you have conducted a legitimate benchmarking analysis, it is critical you remain firm in your resolve and be willing to advocate on your behalf. As soon as you begin to question your value or the relative BATNA strength of the parties, the concessions will start flowing and you will achieve a sub-optimal result.

6. **Are you using the right sources to develop your benchmark?** Historically, comparing salaries with your friends or co-workers was taboo. But with the arrival of the millennials in the workforce and the free exchange of all personal information on social media, that dynamic has changed completely. I encourage you to visit websites such as Indeed.com, Glassdoor.com, PayScale.com, Monster.com, and others where industry and geography specific salary information is readily accessible.

7. **How do you plan on taking maximum advantage of your negotiating position given the current market conditions?** Be mindful of the fact that while the current environment favors the employee, you don't want to be overly confident and overplay your BATNA. Think about whether you will explicitly threaten to leave if you don't get the increase you are seeking. Remember my mom's advice: It's easier to find a job when you have a job. Or put differently, don't put your gun on the table unless it is loaded and you intend to pull the trigger. If you have another job offer in hand AND are prepared to leave, then make that clear. If you are not prepared to leave, I suggest you keep the gun holstered. Once you have placed the

metaphorical gun on the table, two things will occur: (1) you will either be shown the door; or (2) your boss will acquiesce and match the competing offer. If it is the later, your relationship will likely be poisoned forever and future opportunities for advancement will be minimized. In my experience, holding your boss or employer hostage for more money is not a good long-term strategy. Everyone I have seen pursue this approach generally gets the increase but sacrifices long term success.

8. **Have you timed your request properly?** Has the annual budget for the coming year been finalized?

9. **Have you timed your request with the performance of your organization?** If the company is performing well, then the likelihood of success is much greater. Do your homework in this area. Review financial statements and other SEC filings if your company is publicly traded, or review internal communications regarding financial performance to which you have access.

INTERESTS—I WANT IT MY WAY

Now that you have a general understanding of the amount of salary increase you want and the factors that may come into play during the negotiation, let's discuss interests. Interests are defined as the needs, concerns, goals, hopes, and fears that motivate parties to negotiate. To be successful in any negotiation, you must clearly document the interests of the parties, identify any interests that are shared, different, or in conflict, and analyze priorities. Most importantly, you must focus on interests and not positions. In discussing interests with the other party, here are general guidelines for success:

1. Prioritize the interests of the other party—don't assume you know what the party wants or needs.

2. Identify any common interests that you have with the other party.

3. Identify any conflicting interests you have with the other party.

4. Think about the duration of the interests? Are they all short term? Long term? Can the time focus be adjusted to develop more common interests?

5.   Are all the interests purely financial in nature? Are they organizational or personal?

6.   Ask for tradeoffs among the various interests instead of trying to force your interests on the other party.

7.   Prepare as diligently as possible.

8.   Use inquiry to your advantage—do not advocate.

9.   Listen carefully—seek to understand.

As I discussed previously, positions are statements of what a party will or will not do and are conclusions formed before the negotiation even begins. Positions are focused on satisfying the interests of one party and result in the other party reacting in one of two ways—fight or flight. Fighters say it is my way or the highway, which often leads to games of chicken with disastrous and undesirable results. Those who choose the flight option leave the table and pursue their alternative.

Good negotiators make every effort to understand the interests of all parties. However, less successful negotiators fight over positions, quickly reach an impasse, and either walk away from the table or reach a flawed agreement. These negotiators are so focused on position that they haven't taken the time to fully understand the interests of the other party. They approach the negotiation as haggling over opening positions, fighting to reach the best and final positions, and playing a game of concessions that is likely to result in "splitting the difference" and leaving plenty of waste on the table.

When you are entering your boss's office to secure your raise, your primary interest is clear: you want to get the salary increase to which you believe you are legitimately entitled. You may also have a number of other interests which, based upon your prioritization, will be considered when evaluating options that meet your primary interest. Those interests may include keeping a good working relationship with your boss; maintaining forward momentum in your career path, including any future promotions that may be in the pipeline; being viewed as a valued employee who delivers results; expanding your knowledge in a particular functional area, technology, industry, or market; limiting the amount of stress in your life; feeling happy and satisfied with your job; or having a sense of confidence that you work in an environment where you are treated fairly.

Although you will not fully understand your boss's interests until you cross the threshold of her office, you can expect her interests to be these: rewarding you with a salary increase that she believes is market-relevant, consistent with similarly situated employees in her management control performing similar duties; operating in accordance with organizational compensation policy; maintaining a good working relationship with her employees and her boss; helping her employees be successful; maintaining compliance with any financial policies; delivering in accordance with any budgetary or other performance targets for which she is held accountable and upon which her compensation is predicated; limiting the amount of stress in her life; and feeling happy and satisfied with her job.

It is also important to consider the interests of your boss and determine if her interests are consistent with the organization's interests. Although she likely shares a broad interest in delivering against the overall mission of the organization, she may have a key interest in achieving some sales, budgetary, or other personal performance metric that may conflict with the organization's interests in your satisfaction regarding salary.

Based upon the list of interests above, there may be both common and competing interests, and the time sensitivity of those interests may vary. I recommend that you are mindful of where you share common interests and identify options that meet those common interests. When doing so, I also recommend you consider options that may be of low cost to you but yield high gains for the other party. Just remember that the annual review process and pilgrimage to the boss's office is something that occurs every day in workplaces around the world, so finding those shared interests and solving this negotiation puzzle can be achieved.

Although I advocate identifying shared interests, I want you to be in compete mode when you enter the boss's office. You are going to focus on developing an option that satisfies your interests well and that satisfies the interests of your boss and employer in an acceptable or tolerable way. Forget about win-win and smiles all around the table. Those can be saved for transactions in which you are not involved.

OPTIONS—UNDER WHAT CONDITIONS MIGHT YOU SAY YES?

Developing options is a crucial, if not the most important, component of being a successful negotiator. It is essential to keep an open mind, think outside the box, wear your creative hat, and stick to this principle: Rather than saying no, under what conditions might you say yes? Do not get too attached to a particular option, especially one you are most comfortable with based upon precedent. Just because you've been doing something a particular way for a long time doesn't mean it's not incredibly stupid.

Options are possible ways to satisfy the interests of the parties. The measuring stick for evaluating an option is whether it will result in an agreement that leaves no joint benefits on the table, is the best of many options, and meets everyone's interests at some level. It is not simply splitting the difference. Remember that options—unlike alternatives, which are things you do away from the table or where you go when you walk away—originate at the table, with your bottom line being the least acceptable option that you would accept.

When you are in doubt, I want you to think about little Jack and Jill who were arguing over the orange. They agreed to split the orange and in doing so created nothing but an undesirable agreement with unrealized benefits. Had they taken the time to understand each other's interests, they could have invented an option for their mutual gain. So please, under no circumstance should you ever agree to split oranges. Let's take a look at how that might sound in your boss's office during the salary negotiation:

Employee: I have done a lot of market research regarding my current compensation level. I have looked at positions similar to mine at many of our key competitors and elsewhere in the marketplace. I have focused on individuals with similar years of experience, educational backgrounds, and technical certifications. That research consistently indicates that my base salary is well below the market average. I also continue to overachieve on my performance targets and have done so on a consistent basis for the past three years. Given the legitimate market data I referenced, which I have copied for our discussion today, I am seeking a base salary increase of 10% or $10,000.

Boss: While the $10,000 may be consistent with the market data you gathered, it is simply too high and beyond my approval authority. Increases of that size will also detrimentally impact the annual budget.

Employee: My performance justifies an increase of that magnitude as does the market data I have gathered. Given that you will be able to increase my client billing rate in an amount consistent with the increase, it should be budget-neutral.

Boss: Let me go and check with my manager and with Human Resources. I will get back with you this afternoon.

A few hours pass…

Boss: I spoke with my manager and with Human Resources and the maximum salary increase we can offer is $5,000.

Employee: Well, I am at $10,000. What do you say we simply split the difference and agree to $7,500?

Boss: Let me make a quick call.

A few minutes pass.

Boss: OK. We can agree to $7,500.

In this scenario, the employee clearly did some homework and his salary demand was grounded in legitimacy. He knew the market relevant salary data for similarly situated individuals performing in a similar capacity. He also knew—as did his boss—that any salary increase would have been predominantly recovered in the form of a higher billing rate. However, despite the overabundance of legitimacy and what appeared to be some common shared interests, the employee and the boss set aside legitimacy and agreed to split oranges. Ultimately, the employee agreed to a sub-optimal increase of $2,500 less than requested that was not grounded in legitimacy and which he will likely regret as soon as he gets back to his desk.

Neither party spent any time discussing legitimate options—staggering the increase over the course of the calendar year and maximizing recoverability; additional paid time off; a more flexible work schedule; tuition reimbursement or specialized training on a particular technology; or a bonus based upon mutually agreement performance targets.

If the parties had addressed these options, they could have dealt with the variation and could have gotten real value. The employee, however, rushed to judgment to his detriment and did not even think about pursuing his alternative. The employee could have very easily gotten up out of the chair and told his boss he wanted the matter escalated. Or at a minimum that while he appreciated the $5,000 offer, he wanted to discuss other potential options by which the full $10,000 increase could be satisfied. Instead, he felt Velcroed to his seat and folded like a lawn chair. If the employee knew that $10,000 was a market-relevant and legitimate salary increase, then why deviate from that number?

How many times have you been involved in a negotiation where you believe you have deadlocked with the other party? Have you felt trapped with no apparent way forward? This is the turning point in a negotiation. You will either act like an inexperienced negotiator and compromise or split the difference, leaving both parties unhappy or dissatisfied. Or, you will act like a principled, disciplined, and experienced negotiator by refusing to haggle like fishmongers and, consequently, break the deadlock. To do so, you will seek out the interests behind the parties' positions. You will think creatively to identify new possibilities and new concepts grounded in legitimacy. Then you should be able to identify an option that will optimize both parties' outcomes or at least improve one party's well-being without harming the other. After doing that, you should be able to move forward to an agreement.

When engaging in the salary increase negotiation, the options are extensive given the number of variables that can be utilized to satisfy the demand. If an impasse is reached similar to what occurred in the above scenario, consider the following options:

1. A one-time performance bonus

2. A recurring bonus tied to the achievement of a series of objective, measurable, and verifiable performance targets

3. A more flexible schedule—working from home, working four days a week, or more flexible hours

4. More paid time off or even unlimited time off

5. Payment for dues in a professional or other affinity organization

6. Tuition reimbursement

7. Fees for specialized training—a course or certification program

8. Reimbursement for transportation expenses—parking or mass transit

9. Reimbursement for gym or club membership initiation fees or dues

10. Enhanced insurance benefits

11. A sabbatical to pursue a personal interest

12. A contribution to the charity of your choice

13. A stock option or restricted share grant with an accelerated vesting schedule

14. Reimbursement for an airline club membership or other travel perks—ability to book in first class for flights over three hours

15. Placement on a high impact or high-profile assignment

16. Assignment of a mentor that will take an active role in your career advancement

17. A change in title

18. Assuming additional responsibilities or an enhanced leadership role

19. A more attractive office location

20. Invitations to certain company-sponsored sporting or other events—Super Bowl, Formula One Race, etc.

As you can see, there is a lengthy list of options that can be considered to satisfy the salary increase. As discussed previously, the utilization of these options will vary depending on a variety of factors including your age, tenure, time of year, and career aspirations. Before you create waste and split the difference, think about all the possible options by which the mutual interests of the parties can be satisfied. It is the failure to engage in this exercise that derails many negotiations.

Finally, options must be considered in light of the relative BATNA strength of the parties. Remember, options originate at the table; alternatives happen away from the table. I will discuss alternatives later in this book, but please don't assume, like many employees do, that your alternatives are weak when seeking a salary increase.

LEGITIMACY—IN GOD WE TRUST...
ALL OTHERS BRING DATA

Legitimacy is defined as how much an agreement is fair, wise, or sensible as measured by objective, measurable, and verifiable criteria. Overall, legitimacy may include researching industry practices, expert opinions, laws, rules, regulations, precedent, standard procedures, and community standards.

Although the Rebel Negotiator believes that each element in a negotiation is important, legitimacy ranks at the top of the list. Think about positions and interests. It is very easy to establish a subjective one-sided position not grounded in reality well before the negotiation even begins. As I pointed out, positional negotiation quickly ends in fight or flight, neither of which is ideal. If the parties can identify interests and generate options, those options must be legitimate. If the other party refuses to negotiate fairly, the encounter is likely to be brief.

Unlike a car purchase negotiation where an optimal result can generally be well defined, the desired outcome for a salary negotiation can be highly ambiguous given the level of legitimate salary data that may be available to both parties. Historically, legitimate and actual salary data was only available to your employer. As we have discussed, that trend continues to change as salary data becomes more readily available. The more general availability of salary data clearly favors the employee in a salary negotiation. In the car buying transaction, the purchase price of a new car has clear guardrails which come in the form of the sticker and invoice price for the vehicle as well as plenty of the data from Internet searches that will tell you what similar buyers have paid for similar vehicles in your area.

So, before you even step into the dealership, you have a strong understanding of the zone of potential agreement (ZOPA) of the parties. This zone is the space between your bottom line—the last option you will accept before you go to your alternative—and the dealership's bottom line—the last option it will accept before it goes to its alternative.

With the salary negotiation, we do not have such clearly defined guardrails and our ZOPA may vary accordingly. *The zone of potential agreement is illustrated in Figure 8.*

FIGURE 8

HOW WIDE IS THE ZOPA?

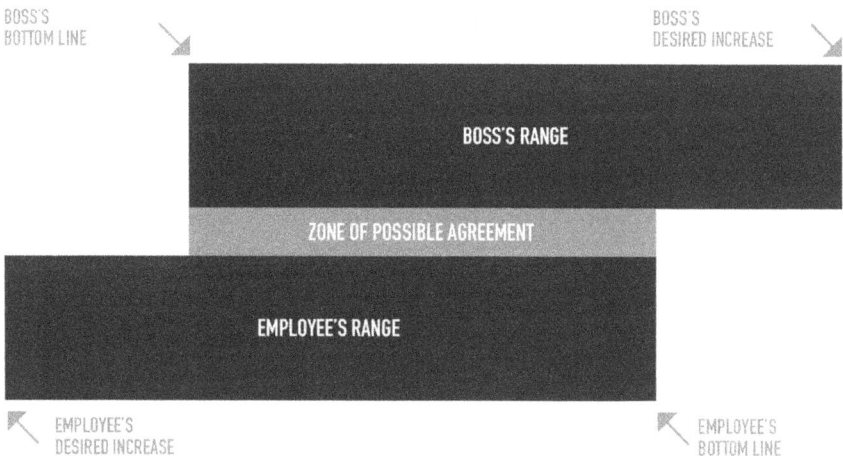

BOSS'S BOTTOM LINE

BOSS'S DESIRED INCREASE

BOSS'S RANGE

ZONE OF POSSIBLE AGREEMENT

EMPLOYEE'S RANGE

EMPLOYEE'S DESIRED INCREASE

EMPLOYEE'S BOTTOM LINE

Each party's bottom line will be determined by the party's interests, the options that meet those interests, and legitimacy. In the salary increase context, legitimacy is based on objective and measurable data from these sources:

1.   Websites that include job postings and salary data for roles like the one in which you are engaged including Indeed.com, Glassdoor.com, Payscale.com, Monster.com, and LinkedIn.com

2.   Social Media websites where personal data of all types is commonplace

3.   Job postings and corresponding salary ranges on competitor websites

4.   Feedback from similarly situated colleagues that are serving in similar positions in your geography

5.   Conversations with recruiters about current roles and salary ranges for which they have been retained

6.   Securities and Exchange Commission and other governmental or public filings that contain compensation data

7.   Internal company data that reflects compensation practices, position descriptions, and salary bands

The salary negotiation experience has evolved considerably, given the vast amounts of data available online. Both employers and employees can refer to data that will provide legitimacy and serve as an objective measuring stick. With that data in hand, the parties can identify options that meet their interests and be the basis for any subsequent agreement and commitment. Although most legitimacy is objective, subjectivity is possible given the potential bias of the parties. I strongly encourage you to use and maximize legitimacy to create a zone of potential agreement for the parties. If you discover you aren't in this zone—an option better than your bottom line—or you believe that the options are unfair or not based in legitimacy, then take a deep breath and pursue your alternative.

ALTERNATIVES—NO VELCRO ALLOWED

I am now ready to talk about alternatives or your best alternative to a negotiated agreement (BATNA). Options originate at the negotiating table, while alternatives occur when you act unilaterally without the other party's agreement. Your BATNA is where you go when you walk away from the table; you can choose to go to your BATNA at any time during the negotiation.

As I discussed in the prior book in this series, your BATNA will never be stronger than when you are buying a new car, and you should never feel entrapped when engaged in that negotiation. You simply get up from the chair where you're sitting, grab the water and whatever may be left of your Otis Spunkmeyer cookies, and head calmly to the exit.

Unfortunately, when negotiating a salary increase with your boss, your BATNA may not be nearly as strong. But to be clear, please don't underestimate your BATNA, as doing so will undermine the integrity of your negotiation approach and strategy. I can't tell you how many times I have watched seasoned executives prepare diligently for a negotiation and carefully evaluate the respective BATNA strength of the parties. Even if that analysis reflects that they have a stronger BATNA than the other party, they forget that fact before they get settled in their chair and well, I am sure you can envision what happens next—decisions are made based upon fear and sub-optimal results are achieved. The entire 4x7 approach we have discussed requires you to remain principled and disciplined in the negotiation and to be mindful of the BATNA strength of the parties coming into the negotiation and as it evolves during the negotiation. If you fail to remain calm, principled, and disciplined, then you might as well forgo the negotiation and go play golf.

To recap, it is your ultimate objective to engage in an effective negotiation. In other words, you can successfully communicate with the other party and maintain a good working relationship. Doing this should help you to uncover the interests of the parties; these interests lead to beneficial, legitimate options that create value for both parties. In many negotiations, this approach yields an option that meets the parties' interests, and an agreement can be reached. However, that is not always the case and you may realize it is better to walk away and go to your BATNA—the best alternative to a negotiated agreement.

BATNA is based on the premise that any agreement with another party must be better than your alternative. That concept makes perfect sense in theory but is much more difficult to follow in practice. Going to BATNA, or even thinking about it, is very difficult for many parties and requires strong discipline. Despite that fear and anxiety, it is crucial that before you enter into a negotiation, you identify your BATNA and the BATNA of the other party. Once you know your BATNA, you may need to disclose it during the negotiation in either a threatening or nonthreatening way, and reality-test the legitimacy of the other party's BATNA. Your mission, should you choose to accept it, is to improve your BATNA during the negotiation and legitimately weaken the BATNA of the other party.

Always know your BATNA before the negotiation begins. When you find yourself sitting in the chair in your boss's office with her raising all sorts of reasons why the amount of raise you seeking is unreasonable and proposing that you split the difference, knowing your BATNA is critical. If you can't agree on the terms of a raise with your boss and your request is grounded in legitimacy, and you have exhausted all possible options, then you must go to your BATNA. It is then that you must exercise absolute discipline.

I realize that going to your BATNA in this context is not as easy as going to the car dealership on the other side of town. Leaving a job is a significant decision and the stakes are high; that is why it is critical that you prepare and strictly adhere to the 4x7 methodology. As you prepare for the negotiation and think about strengthening your BATNA before the negotiation begins, remember my mom's perspective that it is easier to look for a job when you have a job. So, if your BATNA is going to work for a competitor, execute against that strategy well before you enter your boss's office. Having an offer in hand, even if you don't intend to mention or accept it, will reinforce your level of discipline and keep you from feeling entrapped in the salary negotiation.

Before I get into a specific BATNA analysis for your salary negotiation experience, let's discuss the general principles of BATNA. They are as follows:

1. **BATNA is not constant.** Alternatives change over time. Just because you have an iron-clad BATNA on Day 1 of the negotiation does not mean that it can't deteriorate by Day 20. The same applies to the other party; he may have a strong BATNA on Day 1 and may assert his BATNA early and often. Remember that BATNA strength may ebb and flow significantly during the negotiation.

2. **Personal and organizational BATNA may conflict.** Always know the difference between personal BATNA and organizational BATNA. In the salary negotiation context, is the BATNA of your employer the same as that of your boss? Think about how a disparity between personal and organizational BATNA may affect the negotiation.

3. **BATNA is a dangerous weapon.** Be careful when you assert your BATNA, as the other party can perceive it as a threat. If you do throw it out there, be prepared for the other side to test its legitimacy.

4. **Once you pull the trigger, BATNA, like a bullet, is in**

motion. If you are going to assert your BATNA and leave the table, then you must be ready to do so and accept 100 percent of the consequences.

5. **You are free to leave at any time.** Neither party should ever feel entrapped in the negotiation. Both parties have a decision to make and any agreement should be better than their alternative. If it is not, then walking away is a reasonable and prudent decision.

6. **At what point will you walk away?** It is important to distinguish between your bottom line—the least acceptable option that you will agree to—and pursuing your alternative. Remember that options are ideas that originate at the negotiating table, whereas alternatives are unilateral actions you can take away from the table without the other party's consent or participation.

7. **Preparation is critical.** Know your bottom line and BATNA before you start negotiating. Do you have some minimum raise that you absolutely can't do without? Do you need to receive a certain amount in cash compensation? Can you accept the remainder through other means? Again, you have to know the point at which you believe you have exhausted all possible options that will fulfill your interests and then head for the door.

8. **How strong is your BATNA?** Think carefully about your BATNA strength versus that of the other party and how that disparity may affect your negotiation strategy. Think of these scenarios:

   a. **Both parties have a strong BATNA:** If both parties have a strong BATNA, then the question becomes, "so what now?" Since both parties have a viable place to walk to if they can't reach an agreement, this should help facilitate an effective negotiation based on honest, open, and candid communication. In the salary negotiation context, I accept a job at another employer and my employer replaces me with a new hire.

b. **You have a strong BATNA and the other party has a weak BATNA:** What should you do? Be as aggressive as possible and take the other party to the cleaners? I will leave this choice to your discretion. Think of how your actions may affect a long-term relationship. Unlike with a car salesman, you likely do care about the relationship you will have with your boss after this negotiation is completed. Taking advantage of the situation is probably not the best course of action either as many future non-salary related negotiations will likely ensue in which your BATNA may not be so strong and the last thing you want is someone with an axe to grind.

c. **You have a weak BATNA and the other party has a strong BATNA:** The other party will be going through the same analysis in Scenario B above. What will you do? Cave in? Grovel? While this scenario is certainly possible in the salary negotiation context, think about the result. Worst case scenario, your boss tells you that no increase is available or agrees to one that is far less than you are seeking and there is nothing else she can do. If there are no other options that meet your interests, then you thank her for the time and likely get back to work. You can then either do nothing—which is always a viable alternative—or immediately begin your job search.

d. **Both parties have a weak BATNA:** This is when you should exercise extreme caution. In the salary context, this would be an instance in which you are unable to find another job and your employer is unable to hire a replacement. If this scenario occurs, you are likely going to be playing a game of chicken and that never ends well.

Hopefully, when you attempt to secure a salary increase, you will find yourself in Scenario A where both parties have a reasonably strong BATNA. The employee is likely to have a reasonably strong BATNA given the multitude of employment opportunities that exist in the marketplace. Given the current "war" for talent, opportunities seem to abound for individuals with the right experience, professional accomplishments, technical certifications, or security clearance. In addition, technology has facilitated the ability to easily connect with peers and find new opportunities that are consistent with your background and skillset. Of course, this assumes you have desirable skills and you are a reasonably strong performer.

The employer is likely to have a reasonably strong BATNA given its ability to hire a replacement in a timely manner, to promote someone from within the organization to assume your job responsibilities, to off-shore your obligations to someone in a lower cost geography, or to potentially automate many of the routine tasks in which you were engaged. Even in an environment in which unemployment levels are at historically low levels, the applicant pool seems flush with candidates who are just entering the workforce or looking to move from their current employer. Of course, this assumes that the required skills for your position are generally available in the marketplace and that the cycle time to fill the position is minimal.

The likelihood of finding yourself in Scenario A will certainly change based upon the answer to several questions including:

1. What if you have a unique set of skills that are not readily available in the marketplace?

2. What if you have a set of skills that are highly fungible and easily replaceable?

3. What if you have extensive institutional knowledge that

your employer simply can't let walk out the door?

4. What if you oversee a large group of employees who worship your leadership skills and who would revolt if you were to leave?

5. What if you have a competing job offer in your hand that will pay you in a manner consistent with the salary increase you are seeking?

6. What if you are grossly overpaid in relation to market?

7. What if you are a consistent top performer?

8. What if you are a consistent poor performer?

9. What if you have strong relationships in key client accounts who might rethink their customer loyalty if you left?

10. What if you were about to close a strategic transaction that will have significant financial impact in the coming quarter?

11. What if you have stock options or other restricted shares that don't vest until next year?

12. What if the company is going to go public in 18 months and all of your options and restricted shares will immediately vest?

13. What if you only have three more years until retirement?

14. What if you have thirty more years until retirement?

15. What if you have a family to support and leaving one employer without a firm offer elsewhere is not feasible?

16. What if all your close friends, spouse, or significant other work for the same employer?

17. What if your boss has been in your regular golfing foursome for the past five years?

18. What if you work for the largest employer in the city in which you reside?

19. What if you just really like your current job?

20. What if you have a limited professional network and don't interview well?

21. What if you simply are averse to any kind of substantive change?

The answers to these types of questions will certainly impact the BATNA strength of the parties as you enter the salary negotiation. In addition to these questions, let's do a general BATNA analysis for both the employee and employer as we enter the salary negotiation:

Employee BATNA:

1. Do nothing. Accept the fact you can't get the increase you are seeking. The gap between the increase you were seeking and what your boss agreed to is simply not significant enough to pursue a change in employment. Maybe she will come back and increase the offer.

2. Immediately commence the search for a new job.

3. Pick up the phone and accept the new job offer you have already secured.

4. Escalate the matter beyond your immediate boss to her

superior, to Human Resources, to a mentor, or anyone else who may assist you in securing the raise you are seeking. Please do so with caution as this will likely impact your relationship with your boss. If your options are die at her hand, or go around her, then you may not have a choice.

5. Secure another job offer in writing and present that offer to your boss. Tell her to match it or you are leaving.

6. Accept the lower salary increase and do less—stop working on the weekend, stop reading email at all hours of the day and night, identify and adhere to stronger lines of demarcation around the work day. Stop being an over-achiever. For some of you, especially those who like to compete, this may be easier said than done, and execution of this alternative will likely vary depending upon your age, tenure, and timeline to retirement.

7. Retire if you can do so.

8. Develop an action plan with a series of performance targets, that if achieved, will serve as legitimacy for the increase you are seeking during the next performance evaluation cycle.

9. Talk to peers or search job postings in other operating groups or divisions of your employer. Pursue a transfer that may come with the salary increase you are seeking.

10. Pursue a new degree or technical certification that will equip you with the skills required for a new role or assignment that has a richer compensation plan.

11. Devote all of the time you are saving in alternative #6 to your friends, family, health, or a charity. While getting more money may be desirable, the time invested in these areas is priceless.

12. Give your employer two weeks' notice and figure out your next move when you wake up the next morning. Though I won't advise against this alternative, I will remind you again of what my mom says about how much easier it is to find a job while you have a job. If you question this perspective, think about your BATNA strength when negotiating salary and terms with a potential new employer when you have been unemployed for three or six months.

13. Start that new venture you have been thinking about for years. Stay in your current job and focus on the new venture in your free time. You will know when it is time to make a formal change.

14. Propose an incentive-based performance plan to your boss based upon the achievement of certain objective, measurable, and verifiable milestones during the upcoming year.

15. Get a part-time job to make up the income gap you are trying to close.

Employer BATNA:

1. Promote a replacement from within the organization.

2. Hire an external candidate.

3. Do nothing and wait for the employee to react to the offer on the table. Maybe he will accept the proposed terms.

4. Do nothing even if the employee leaves. Refrain from backfilling the role. Segregate the responsibilities among existing staff or deploy more automation or off-shore to a lower cost geography.

Based upon this analysis, I would prefer to be on the side of the employee. Always remember your BATNA when you enter your boss's office for this discussion. Don't get entrapped. Don't underestimate the strength of your BATNA. Remain principled and disciplined. Focus on legitimacy. Remember, you are not Velcroed in the chair. If your boss or employer won't agree to an option that meets your interests, sit up, take a deep breath, and be prepared to execute your BATNA if necessary.

COMMITMENT—ARE YOU AUTHORIZED TO MAKE THAT DECISION?

A commitment is a statement or a binding promise that reflects a party's obligations. Good commitments are realistic, well planned, free from ambiguity, and can be implemented or executed against. There are three types of commitments in a negotiation. First, there is the parties' commitment to the process of the negotiation. Second, there is the commitment to an option that meets the parties' interests. Third, there is a commitment at the end of the negotiation to formalize the parties' commitment and to execute their obligations in the agreement.

When arriving at the meeting to discuss your salary increase, I encourage you to get a commitment to the process of the negotiation. From the employee's perspective, the sooner the negotiation concludes, the better. So I recommend you set a time limit on the duration of the negotiation.

You must make it clear that you say what you mean, and you mean what you say. If you commit to two hours, then that is the timeline you'll work in. Remember, your boss wants to keep you in that seat as long as possible, wear you out, refute the legitimacy upon which your increase is predicated, and make you feel entrapped. If you've carefully read this book, you will not fall for that tactic.

When you've agreed on a process, it is time to communicate interests and discuss options. I encourage you to be as direct as possible with your boss about the amount of the increase you are seeking. Don't be afraid to clearly articulate the legitimacy upon which the increase you are seeking is predicated. Be clear with your interests and be flexible regarding options by which those interests can be met. If you can find an option that meets your interests, you can move forward to the next stage of commitment. If you can't find an acceptable option, then you may need to assert—either in a subtle or direct manner—your BATNA. Whatever you do, do not split oranges and do not be afraid to assert and execute your BATNA.

One key component of the second stage of commitment is the authority of the parties conducting the negotiation. Although you might be feeling some pressure from a third party who has a vested interest in your raise, I will assume you are fully empowered and authorized to reach an agreement. As you discuss the various options with your boss, it is possible she will have to seek approval from some third party, either her boss, Human Resources, or the finance organization to finalize the terms of your increase, especially if it includes some non-cash components. While your boss is likely empowered to commit on behalf of your employer, she may not have complete authority to do so without seeking some other approvals.

Unlike your car purchase transaction where I encourage you to simply bypass the salesperson and negotiate directly with the sales manager, it is not as easy to do so when you are negotiating with your boss. You don't want to disrespect her authority and you need to be mindful of the fact that going around her to achieve a better outcome will likely have a detrimental impact on your long-term relationship. With that said, if your boss lacks the authority to agree with your request, then you may need to engage another party in the process to achieve the result you are seeking. In the car buying context, I would say why waste time negotiating with someone who lacks the power to commit to price or terms? In the salary increase context, you will need to display some level of diplomacy. If your boss lacks the authority to commit to an option that meets your interests, then it makes sense to engage the individual who has the proper level of authority to help facilitate a timely and efficient result. To the extent you have a strong relationship with your boss, engaging that third party might facilitate an objective outcome that is not influenced by the relationship. More importantly, doing so may minimize any detrimental impact on your relationship. Now if your boss lacks authority and is unwilling to engage someone that does, you may need to go around her to achieve a desired result.

Remember our BATNA analysis. Please be confident as you begin the negotiation. As a valued employee, you have a strong BATNA. You should not feel compelled or forced to do anything. If your boss refuses to negotiate with you or you don't like her attitude, maybe you should consider your BATNA. Do not split oranges, do not compromise, do not accept an option that doesn't fulfill your interests, and do not get entrapped. Know your BATNA, assert your BATNA, and exercise your BATNA freely. If you're afraid, roll play the negotiation with a spouse, significant other, or colleague.

The final stage of commitment will come after you have agreed to terms that meet your interests. If the increase being proposed by your employer does not meet your interests, then go to your BATNA. Once you have agreed on the terms, execute any necessary paperwork, and get back to work. Continue to perform and deliver and be prepared to do the exact same thing during your next annual performance assessment.

The final word is: Don't be in a rush to make a commitment. Slow down, listen for interests, and think about options. Once there is an option that meets your interests, you can agree and make a commitment. Don't get entrapped and don't split the difference in any circumstance.

A BLUE-RIBBON RECIPE

I want to make it clear that the negotiation framework I have previously described applies to all negotiators, regardless of gender. According to research from Carnegie Mellon University, women do not assume as many things are negotiable and miss opportunities to negotiate. They see negotiation as conflict and avoid negotiations completely, struggle in ambiguous situations, and are judged more harshly when they negotiate or advocate on their behalf.

One of the primary reasons why women miss opportunities to negotiate is ascribed to the "asking advantage." This advantage suggests that women worry more than men about the effect their actions will have on their relationships. Ultimately, this results in a desire to protect personal connections, which manifests itself in asking for things indirectly or asking for less.

When I am asked how we can best address the gender differences in negotiation, I point to my recipe for being a successful negotiator because it is gender agnostic. Remember that it is possible to engage in a principled and disciplined negotiation with your boss and at the same time maintain a good working relationship.

A female employee seeking a salary increase, just like her male peer, should not feel anxious, nervous, or stressed upon entering her boss's office for the salary negotiation. Every woman should channel her inner Rebel Negotiator: Be assertive and don't be overly focused on the relationship. Say what you mean and mean what you say. Prepare diligently, focus on interests, consider all options, and maximize legitimacy. Most importantly, remember the strength of your BATNA.

RULES OF THE ROAD

Now that you have read this book, you should be ready to get the salary increase you deserve I will leave you with a list of my key principles and rules of the road that you can quickly refer to when you are in the middle of your negotiation:

1. Never let your relationship with your boss affect your decision-making process.

2. You can always use negative-influence techniques, such as manipulation (lies and deceit), intimidation (loud and abrasive verbal aggressiveness), avoidance (doing nothing), or threats (comply with my desire, or else). But, do so with caution.

3. Don't play games like these: bidding against yourself, positional bargaining that results in compromise, caving in because you feel heavily invested in the process, playing chicken, rewarding anchoring, or making decisions based upon your perceived level of entrapment.

4. Don't assume you have a weak BATNA when seeking a salary increase.

5.   If you don't know your goal, then you might as well call it a day and play golf.

6.   Regarding preparation, remember what Coach Coughlin said: "Humble enough to prepare, confident enough to perform."

7.   Know that the actual negotiation may not flow as smoothly as it did when you role-played in front of the mirror or with your friends, family, or office colleagues.

8.   Temper your approach based upon the amount of risk inherent in the outcome.

9.   Temper your approach base on where you live.

10. Temper your approach based upon the person sitting across from you at the negotiation table.

11. Remember that conflicts are created, conducted, and sustained by human beings, and can be resolved by human beings. It's just an annual salary increase—there's no need to get overly stressed or anxious.

12. Remember the words of Harvey Specter from the television show *Suits*: "What are your choices when someone puts a gun to your head? What are you talking about? You do what they say or they shoot you. WRONG. You take the gun, or you pull out a bigger one. Or, you call their bluff. Or, you do one of a hundred and forty-six other things."

13. As I previously discussed, preparation is an absolute necessity for any negotiation and even more so for delivering a difficult message. I can't stress enough the importance of thorough preparation. Make sure that you have an in-depth understanding of the issues and that you focus on legitimacy.

14. Seek to understand instead of seeking to be understood. The difference may seem subtle, but it is significant and will absolutely affect the tone and tenor of your conversation. Use inquiry instead of advocacy and find the right balance between diplomacy and directness.

15. Prepare yourself for a negative reaction. The conversation may become tense. Your preparation should help you be emotionally ready. Keep your competitive arousal in check—ask yourself, do you want to be right or be effective?

16. Keep things in perspective. How significant are the message and the issue? Will it even matter in six months? In six years?

17. Be a good LIAR—listen, inquire, acknowledge and respond.

18. Once you think you have exhausted the list of potential options, think again. Be open to considering all options; rather than saying no, think about under what conditions you might say yes.

19. Once you cross the threshold of your boss's office, you must follow this rule: You will not let the relationship—real, perceived, or otherwise—influence your decision-making process—period.

20. It's fine to focus on maintaining a good working relationship with your boss, but remember to separate the relationship from the substance of the negotiation.

21. In no circumstance should you ever agree to split oranges.

22. Your BATNA strength when seeking a salary increase is not weak. Under no circumstance should you ever feel entrapped.

23. It is crucial that BEFORE you enter the negotiation you identify your BATNA and the BATNA of the other party.

24. If you are going to assert your BATNA and leave the table, then you must be ready to do so and accept 100 percent of the consequences.

25. It is important to distinguish between your bottom line— the least acceptable option that you will agree to—and pursuing your alternative. Remember that options are ideas that originate at the negotiating table, whereas alternatives are unilateral actions you can take away from the table without the other party's consent or participation.

26. Remain principled and disciplined and focus on legitimacy. You are not Velcroed in the chair. If your boss won't agree to an option that meets your interests, take a deep breath, and be prepared to assert or execute your BATNA.

27. Commit to a process before the negotiation begins.

28. If your boss refuses to negotiate with you or challenges the legitimacy of your demand, you may need to go to your BATNA.

29. Do not split oranges, do not compromise, and do not accept an option that doesn't fulfill your interests.

30. Slow down, listen for interests, and think about options.

31. Female employees should not feel anxious, nervous, or stressed when navigating through this process. Channel your inner Rebel Negotiator. Be assertive and don't overly focus on the relationship. Prepare diligently, focus on interests, consider all options, and maximize legitimacy.

32. Remember, your boss will provide a number of reasons why she can't give you the legitimate salary increase you are seeking. Because you have carefully read this book, you will not fall for her tactics.

Now that you have these key rules and principles, I hope to see you enjoying the influx of cash in your bank account.

ABOUT THE AUTHOR

Grant S. Lange, the Rebel Negotiator, is a Managing Director and member of the Negotiation Center of Excellence for a leading IT and consulting services company and has served in a variety of leadership roles at some of the world's largest IT services, advisory, and software firms. During the day, he is responsible for negotiating large, complex, and strategic consulting, technology, and outsourcing agreements; building trusted adviser relationships with legal, finance, and procurement executives across the *Fortune* 500 client community; developing thought leadership on the art and science of negotiation; and training his colleagues how to fine-tune their negotiation skills. During his career, the Rebel Negotiator has successfully negotiated services agreements that have generated more than $5 billion in new sales.

During his spare time, the Rebel Negotiator rides motorcycles, lifts weights, drives fast cars, and shoots guns. He will always find time to help a colleague, friend, family member, or reader negotiate a raise.

www.ingramcontent.com/pod-product-compliance
Lightning Source LLC
Chambersburg PA
CBHW060626210326
41520CB00010B/1490